THE
MEDIEVAL
KNIGHT

at War

THE MEDIEVAL KNIGHT

at War

BROOKS ROBARDS

TIGER BOOKS INTERNATIONAL
LONDON

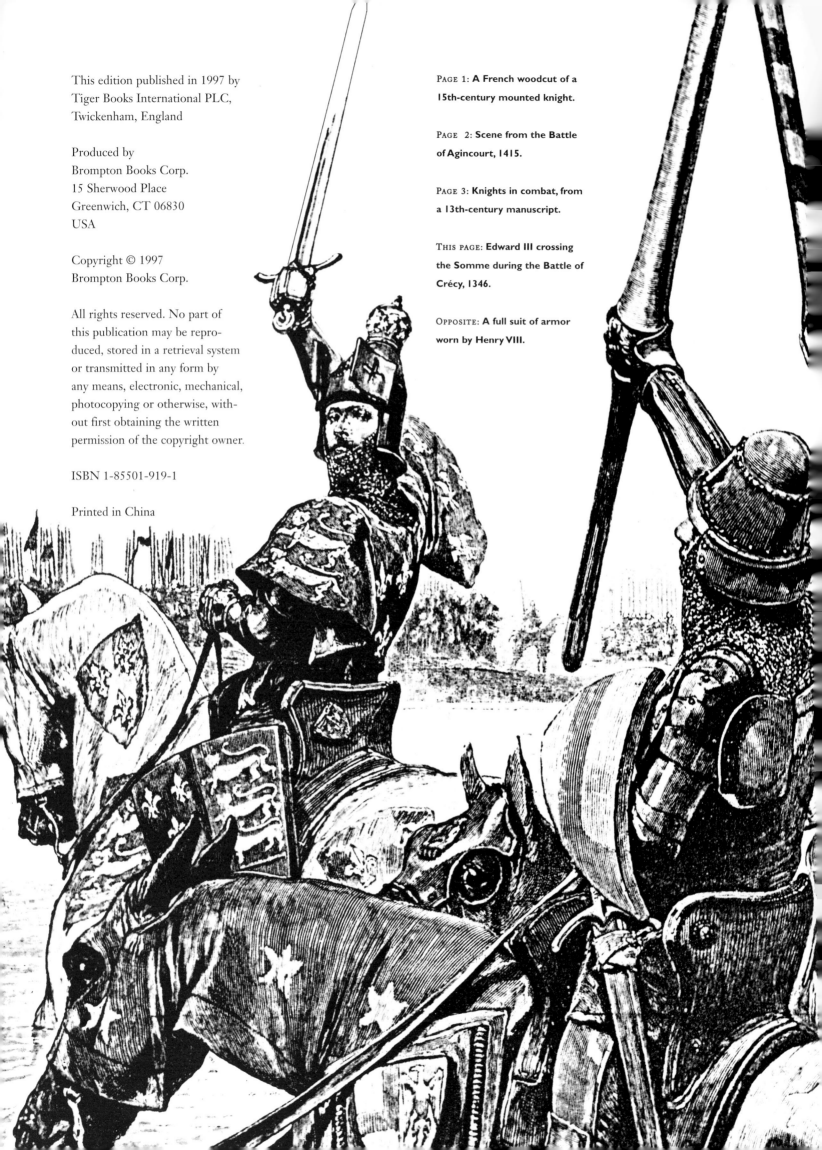

This edition published in 1997 by
Tiger Books International PLC,
Twickenham, England

Produced by
Brompton Books Corp.
15 Sherwood Place
Greenwich, CT 06830
USA

ISBN 1-85501-919-1

Printed in China

PAGE 1: **A French woodcut of a 15th-century mounted knight.**

PAGE 2: **Scene from the Battle of Agincourt, 1415.**

PAGE 3: **Knights in combat, from a 13th-century manuscript.**

THIS PAGE: **Edward III crossing the Somme during the Battle of Crécy, 1346.**

OPPOSITE: **A full suit of armor worn by Henry VIII.**

Contents

The Origins of Knighthood

The word "knight" comes from the Anglo-Saxon word *cniht* or *cnoeht,* meaning young man, youth, or boy. This definition, however, scarcely explains the identity of a knight. The knight was a warrior of the Middle Ages, a fighter who usually rode on horseback and wore armor in a variety of forms, depending on the time period. The best-known knights lived and fought in England and Western Europe from the ninth to the 16th centuries. China and Japan also had their knights, known as samurai in Japan. In the Middle East, knights fought as warriors for the Islamic cause.

Medieval knights were hardly the first soldiers to ride on horses or wear protective armor. Cave drawings dating back thousands of years before the birth of Christ show men riding bareback on horses or reindeer, with bows and arrows in hand. In the heyday of the Roman Empire, legionnaires wore elaborately decorated bronze cuirasses, or torso armor, and helmets with plumes. Yet the warriors of the Middle Ages are probably better remembered than any other fighters in the history of the world. That is because these knights formed an elite military class that operated under a strict and idealistic code of honor, known as chivalry. Knighthood took years of apprenticeship and carried high social rank. The ceremony conducted when a man succeeded to knighthood was often an elaborate ritual and important event in the community.

Knights played an integral part in the prevailing social organization of the time, known as feudalism. Under feudalism, knights pledged the use of their fighting skills to a prince or other powerful leader in exchange for use of a portion of the prince's lands and other property. In this manner, the knight became the prince's vassal or servant. Such a relationship might seem demeaning through modern eyes, but in the Middle Ages it conferred great honor on an individual,

BELOW: **The carved front panel of this 14th-century chest depicts armored Flemish foot soldiers defeating French cavalry at Courtrai in 1302. Carrying mainly swords and clublike pikes, the Flemings showed that, given the right terrain and tactics, infantry could destroy mounted knights.**

OPPOSITE: **A medieval knight on his armored charger.**

because the military obligation mattered far more than the economic one. Eventually, the peasants who worked the land put themselves and their families under the protection of knights, so that knights became responsible for the safety of large communities of people. They formed special brotherhoods or organizations, the most famous of which are the Knights Templars.

The high esteem in which a knight was held because of his fighting skills, and the code of chivalry that guided his life, help to explain the continued fascination we have today for this hero from the past. While the cumbersome protective gear a knight wore — it could weigh as much as 50 pounds — might make him seem like a lumbering anachronism in today's world, modern-day engineers working on the design of space-travel suits for astronauts actually studied medieval suits of armor.

The World Before Knights

To understand who the medieval knight was and what role he played, it is necessary to look briefly at the world in which he lived. By the fifth century A. D., the Roman Empire, which had provided a stable social and political environment in most of Europe and England for nearly 1,000 years, was disintegrating. As the Dark Ages descended, anarchy ruled. Cities fell apart; commerce and industry disappeared. Ordinary citizens were no longer safe in their homes; crops and belongings became subject to pillage by roving bands of "barbarian" marauders. The Roman Empire had essentially been a Mediterranean civilization, located in a region with a mild, dry climate and relatively infertile, slow-growing soil. As Western Europe and England struggled to free themselves from chaos and move forward into the Middle Ages, they were cut off from traditional Mediterranean culture and commerce. The seat of Western civilization shifted north to a geography of deep, heavy soil characterized by dense forests and a wet climate that encouraged rapid growth. The region had originally been populated by Celtic tribes of farmers and cattle-herders. After they left and the Roman Empire collapsed, Germanic tribes were the first to move in and take over. The Germanic invasions undermined existing governmental structures, leaving behind a patchwork of territories ruled by princes and regents without much power. Although the Catholic Church had come to dominate the spiritual

lives of the resident population, it could not provide physical protection for its people, let alone itself. Cathedrals, abbeys and monasteries, the repositories of what wealth remained in the region, were prime targets for looting.

ABOVE: **Danish Vikings disembark from their long ships to attack a headland. Each vessel might carry as many as 50 fighting men, able to do much damage in a short period of time.**

Viking & Moorish Invasions

By the ninth century, bands of Scandinavian scavengers, driven south by overpopulation and the establishment of stable monarchies in their homelands, began to systematically plunder Western Europe and England. They were known as Vikings, a term that did not indicate a place of origin so much as a style of living. Wanderers, adventurers, explorers and pirates, Vikings came from a variety of countries, including Norway, Sweden, and Denmark.

The Vikings kept no written records, which leaves their origins obscured in the mists of time. To learn about them, we must rely on their sagas, written down much later, for information that may not be accurate. Archaeological evidence demonstrates that they were accomplished ship-builders. They traveled in wooden boats more than 70 feet long, powered by oarsmen, and, starting in the ninth century, sails. Initially the Vikings made hit-and-run forays in summer and then headed

BELOW: **A coastal defense force fails to beat off a superior band of Viking raiders. Ultimately, the Vikings were able to range far inland.**

back north with their booty. In time, however, they began to moor their boats offshore or in rivers, and, leaving them under guard, moved inland. Ultimately they set up permanent settlements. The territories of England and Western Europe, fragmented and in decline, were ill-equipped to defend themselves.

While the Vikings were harassing Western Europe from the north, the Moors created a threat from the south through the Spanish peninsula. Inspired by the teachings of Mohammed, who preached the uniting of all Arab peoples under one god Allah, they left the Middle East and struck the Balearic Islands, Sicily, Sardinia, Corsica and southern Italy. Viking settlers in Europe and England had not brought a particularly powerful culture with them, and they tended to absorb the prevailing romanesque traditions. In contrast, the invading nomadic tribes from the Arab countries were driven not by greed but religious passion. Islam taught that if they died in battle against infidels, they would go to paradise. They moved in quickly on horses and camels, using the element of surprise to their advantage. From the east came the Magyars, a people of Mongolian origin related to Huns and Avars.

Like the Moors, they came on horseback in bands, moving in quickly to pillage and then vanishing.

This was the world in which the knight emerged: chaotic, threatened by instant devastation, governed by fear and panic. No real towns were left, the local population was in decline and much cultivated land was reverting to forest. Yet the region had the makings of a mighty civilization in its shared elements — climate, soil, topography, racial structure and culture. Latin, a common language for reading and writing, was one of the important legacies of the Roman Empire.

The experience of living in such a threatening environment led to the development of knighthood. Leaders looked to the creation of a class of soldiers who could stop the invasions. It was clear from the nature of the attacks on Europe and England that two elements above all were necessary to stem the tide of invasions: protective armor and horses.

ABOVE: **This helmet from the Sutton Hoo Ship Burial, seventh century, is derived from the late Roman *spangelhelm*.**

BELOW: **Bronze Age round shields from England. The round design persisted into the 11th century.**

Pre-Knight Armor & Weaponry

The most basic form of armor used by the earliest warriors of the region was the shield. At first it was no more than a loose animal skin held as protection on the non-fighting arm. Then a wooden frame was covered with leather or animal hides, although wicker might be used, particularly in Asia. Eventually the fighter's body and head began to be covered with leather, wicker, padded or quilted cloth and even wood. While iron implements were developed as early as 1500 B.C., iron was at first too costly and rare to be used for protection. In addition, the work involved in hammering out body armor and helmets required a high level of skill and many hours of labor. An alternative was scale armor, consisting of smaller forged plates.

The earliest evidence of mail shirts, constructed of interlinking metal rings, shows up in the Celtic tribes who inhabited England and Western Europe in pre-Roman times. The Roman scholar Varro claimed mail was invented by the Celts, and it first appeared in the Roman Empire in the third century B.C. Mail was the earliest form of body armor worn by Medieval knights. Medieval helmets were adopted from Roman military models, which were rounded or conical.

ABOVE: **A lightly armed**
Breton horseman of 50 B.C.
with sword, lance, and shield.
The horse carried neither
saddle nor stirrups.

The Early Use of Horses

Horses provided warriors with mobility, and that made them important assets to Medieval knights. Just how integral the horse was to knighthood is also demonstrated in the words used to identify this new kind of soldier: chevalier in France; cavaliere in Italy; caballero in Spain; ritter in Germany. Horse rider is the common definition for all of these words. As far back as 1000 B.C., cavalry had been a component of armies, and mounted warriors were always held in high esteem. The Greeks ascribed legendary status to the horseman in the centaur, a mythical mix of man and horse supposed to have lived in Thessaly. The considerable expense of owning, equipping and maintaining horses meant that cavalry was generally confined to royalty and nobility. In both Greece and the Roman Empire, mounted soldiers formed a distinct social class.

The open terrain of central and southwest Asia provided a natural environment for the development of horse-riding military forces as early as 600 B.C. By the time of Philip of Macedonia and Alexander the Great, cavalry horses wore scale-armor headpieces and breastplates. The growing importance of cavalry in

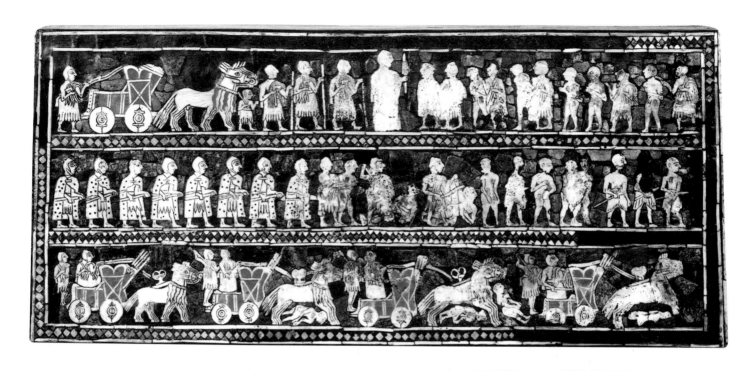

ETSYRIAM SOBAL · ET CONVERTIT
IOAB · ET PERCYSSIT EDOM INVAL
LESALINARVM · XII MILIA ·

battle over time can be attributed to an increase in the use of missile weapons, which thinned out infantry formations and reduced the reliance on hand-to-hand fighting. When infantry formations fanned out, they became particularly vulnerable to cavalry attack.

Critical to the technological advancement of fighting on horseback were the invention of the saddle and stirrup. Development of the saddle, held in place on the horse's back by a girth or strap, gave the soldier a solid seat. First used by Nubian mercenaries from the Nile River valley, the saddle was built high at the pommel in front and at the cantle in back, to keep the rider balanced on the horse's back and in position while fighting. Before the invention of stirrups, warriors rode bareback or were seated on pads or blankets on their horses' backs. Historians say stirrups were first used by Hindu fighters in the first century B.C. Once a mounted soldier could brace his body in a saddle with his feet in stirrups, he was able to fuse his own strength with the force of his steed. This combined power allowed him to impose on his opponent the shock action of his weaponry.

New, heavier breeds of horses from Persia and central Asia reinforced the increased power of shock-action weaponry. By the fourth century A.D., Roman legionnaires were using these heavier horses and covering them with protective coats of mail. People from Asian tribes where horsemanship was traditionally cultivated — Huns, Alans, Avars, Bulgars — had the advantage. Germanic tribes living in the plains region between the Danube and the Black Sea — Goths, Heruli, Vandals, Gepidae, Lombards — also came from a tradition of horsemanship and excelled as cavalrymen. There is debate, however, about how early in the Middle Ages the

OPPOSITE: **A page from a ninth-century Frankish work shows Carolingian cavalry, and is among the earliest depictions of the stirrup.**

ABOVE: **A metal stirrup from the Middle Ages.**

BELOW LEFT: **A drawing from the Triumphal Column of Marcus Aurelius in Rome shows an attack on a rampart by Roman cavalry and shield-protected infantry.**

stirrup began to be used by soldiers and when the changeover to cavalry domination began. In the seventh century, the Lombards were the only Europeans known to use horses widely in battle. So much did they value their steeds that a horse with its harness was valued in Lombard society at twice the worth of a household slave and two-thirds the worth of a simple freeman. For most European and English tribes, though, horses were thought of as pack animals and used primarily for carrying supplies.

In the fifth and sixth centuries — before the advent of knighthood — the northern Teutonic tribe known as the Franks fought almost exclusively on foot. So did the Angles, Saxons and Jutes in England. The extraordinary vitality of the Franks, however, helped them to prevail even against mounted opponents. By the end of the sixth century, the Frankish tribes dominated Western Europe and England. Their encounters with such barbarian invaders as Ostrogoths, Visigoths, Lombards, Avars and East Romans taught them to adopt the use of horses by the seventh century. If knighthood can be said to have had a single origin, it was among the Frankish tribes that overran the western remnants of the Roman Empire, establishing themselves in the region north of the Pyrénées and Alps and west of the Rhine. The Romans called this region Gaul, and we know it as France, a modern spelling of Franks.

It was not a characteristic of the Middle Ages to think in terms of decisive military engagements; it is a modern inclination. But if there was one historical moment when Medieval knighthood began, it was at the Battle of Poitiers in 732 A.D., also known as the Battle of Tours. The Merovingian dynasty of the Frankish Empire — named after the fifth century ruler Merowig — was in the process of disintegrating when Charles Martel came into power and started a new line of strong leaders. Martel, also called Charles the Hammer, is perhaps best known to moderns for lending his name to a brand of fine French cognac.

Administrator or "mayor of the palace" for a Merovingian ruler who had a title but not much power, Martel reunited northern Gaul and re-established Frankish authority in the southern regions of Gaul known as Aquitaine and Burgundy. The Moors, who had already overrun what is now Spain, were making inroads into Gaul when Martel and his army stopped them at Poitiers. Despite his power, Martel never officially became king. His son, Pepin the Short, later became the first Carolingian King of the Franks after succeeding his father as palace mayor. Pepin's rule was legitimated by the Pope. In 800 A.D., Martel's grandson Charlemagne was crowned as the first Emperor of the Holy Roman Empire. The era of the Medieval knight had begun.

ABOVE: In this engraving, Charles Martel brandishes a battle-ax as he leads his lightly armored Franks against the Saracens. The Frankish horses then used for battle were still essentially cart horses.

The Rise of the Knight

Several factors led to the rise of the knight in ninth-century Western Europe. One factor was the tide of invaders, often heathen and always eager to plunder the wealth of the region. Such a tide could not be stemmed on an individual basis by isolated private citizens. A force of specially trained fighters was needed. A second factor was the evolution of a new social order called feudalism. If protection of land and property was going to be accomplished by the new breed of specially trained fighters, there needed to be a supporting system of social organization. The forms of government that followed the break-up of the Roman Empire in Western Europe and England were fragmented, with power divided among a ruler and his followers based on territorial and tribal prerogatives. The glue that held the system together was personal relationships: the charisma of a leader, the loyalty of his followers.

A final factor leading to the appearance of knights had to do with the Roman Catholic Church. The Church saw that an alignment with the leaders of the strongest tribe in the region would allow it to maintain its position of spiritual authority. Serving as the dominant presence in the intellectual and cultural life of Western Europe and England at the time, the Church used its influence to guide the development of knighthood and instill knights with a sense of discipline and holy mission. Through feudalism, it contributed a hierarchy based on the belief that all power comes from God and is delegated temporally on his behalf, whether to priests or rulers or knights.

BELOW: **A gilded bronze masthead weathervane from a Viking ship. The holes along the border are for the attachment of streamers and pendants.**

OPPOSITE: **A Saxon tribal leader agrees to peace under the English King, a first step in the beginning of feudalism and the appearance of a caste of professional warriors, the knights.**

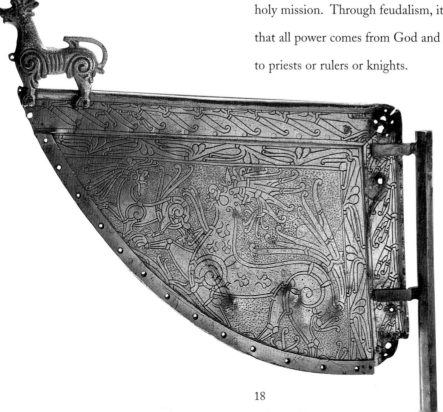

The Threat from Invaders

During the early Middle Ages, life in Western Europe and England was centered on herding and primitive agricultural production. The general population consisted of small communities of people who were dispersed widely and not tied to any central authority. Without adequate means to defend themselves, their families and their resources

TOP: **A relief on an ivory reliquary portrays the Visigoth conquest of northwestern Spain.**

ABOVE: **Visigoths seek refuge from a Saracen onslaught in the mountains of Asturias.**

against invaders, they looked increasingly to the more powerful members of the community for protection.

Even after the Franks — who were to produce the first knights — arrived on the scene and settled, invasions from the North and the East were spearheaded by a variety of other Germanic tribes. Throughout the first millennium, some 20 of these tribes invaded Western Europe and began settling between the Rhine and Elbe rivers. Originally most of them had divided themselves into large family units called kinships. The basic social unit was known as the hundred, and its leader was elected from their midst. Family and tribal ties held these people together and made them a formidable fighting force from the time they were on the move in the days of the Roman Empire. Although untrained as soldiers, most of the Germanic tribes had a reputation for fierce bravery and military effectiveness. When a Roman military unit lost a battle, it dispersed. Not so the Germanic fighters. They operated like an organic body, using squares of 20 men by 20, or 100 men by 100, as their basic tactical formation. The reason they didn't employ the more maneuverable Roman phalanx was simple. The Germans used primitive equipment. They had very little protective armor or metal weaponry. So it was important to concentrate the best-armed fighters at the front of the more compact square formation. An added advantage to the square was that it enabled the fighters to adjust better to the prevailing geography.

Early Germanic Armor & Weapons

Roman historians described early Germanic warriors, including the Franks, fighting bare-chested — even naked — and carrying only brightly painted shields and primitive weapons. Swords were rare. At this stage shields were wooden, with a metal boss, or knob, in the center that had an iron hand grip riveted to it on the inside. Shield colors and bosses served to identify a warrior and his tribe. A warrior's shield was so important that to lose it in battle created the utmost indignity, even leading to suicide. The only worse humiliation was to survive a leader's death in battle.

These early tribesmen didn't have much in the way of material resources, and they developed their own weapons rather than copying Roman models. Most early Germanic fighters carried stones or stone balls with slings to use as missiles. What headgear they had was apt to be made of leather or fur. Many carried iron-headed spears of medium length, called angons, which were similar to the Roman pilum and could be used either to spike or to throw. The iron head of the spear had a barb, which prevented it from being removed once a body was hit. If a warrior embedded his spear in an enemy shield, he could step on the wooden pole, forcing his opponent to drop the shield in which it was implanted and leave him unprotected. The warrior then moved in quickly for the kill.

It is important to remember that Western Europe and England were pre-literate in the early Middle Ages. Unable to leave behind written records, ordinary people often used the important objects in their lives to convey information about themselves. Swords were given names and might be thought to have almost

21

supernatural powers. In the early days, soldiers were buried with their weaponry and implements of war. As a result, churches and grave sites still provide the best resources for modern-day research on early Medieval military armament. While elaborately decorated helms, as helmets were called, swords and other implements have been found in early Frankish graves, body armor has not. Most Germanic soldiers couldn't have afforded body armor, and some historians theorize that it may have been too valuable ever to be buried. A shirt of mail was estimated as equivalent in worth at the time to two horses or two helms.

The special significance of an object such as a sword is illustrated by the following description, written by Theodoric the Ostrogoth's secretary to convey thanks for a gift of swords to the leader from another tribal chief:

> Your fraternity has chosen for us swords capable even of cutting through armor,
> which I prize more for their iron than for the gold upon them. So resplendent is their
> polished clarity that they reflect with faithful distinctness the faces of those who look
> upon them . . . . The central part of their blades, cleverly hollowed out, appears to be
> grained with tiny snakes, and here such varied shadows play that you would believe
> the shining metal to be interwoven with many colors.

ABOVE: **A rendering of the battle dress and weapons of early Germanic tribesmen. Most headgear was of leather or fur, and there was very limited use of costly metal body armor.**

The Advent of the Franks

Of the collection of heathen German tribes who invaded Western Europe and England, one group stood out: the Franks. They first colonized Western Europe in the fourth century through an alliance with the Roman Empire. It was the job of the Franks, led by their princes, to keep other barbarian tribes at bay for the Empire. In exchange they were allowed to settle without being attacked by the Romans. Unlike the Goths, Lombards or Vandals, the Franks embraced Christianity. That was to prove an important difference. The Franks' first great king, Clovis, had himself baptized at the beginning of the sixth century, and his rule gained further credibility when the Roman Emperor gave him a crown and robe in 508 A.D.

The early social organization of the Germanic tribes, reflected in the military structure of the square with its familial closeness and democratically elected leader, gradually disappeared as the Franks became the dominant tribe in Western Europe. Power passed from the general populace to Frankish kings, who led the tribes' fighting sorties and reaped the biggest rewards in booty. Gradually, those who served as members of a king's war party became administrators for his household, along with the land and properties he accumulated. The head of these administrators was called the Mayor of the Palace.

The Emergence of Feudalism

The hierarchical structure that came from the Roman Catholic Church and would develop into feudalism was put into operation by the Franks. Unlike the Ostrogoths, Visigoths and Vandals, the Franks absorbed the native Gauls into their ranks when they settled in their territory. Relying in part on the territorial divisions set up during the Roman Empire, the Frankish kings delegated governing power over

CLOVIS. I.

ABOVE: **Clovis I, King of the Salian Franks, brought a form of unity to the northern Frankish tribes.**

BELOW LEFT: **The baptism by Gallic churchmen of Clovis, first Christian King of the Franks. In Clovis, the Roman Catholic Church found a defender against barbarian invaders.**

much of their kingdom to their counts. As the amount of territory under royal control increased, dukes were put in charge of groups of counts, particularly in strategic border regions. Administrative responsibility did not need to be held exclusively by individuals of Frankish birth — let alone be limited to individuals with family ties — but might include Romans, Gauls and other freemen. This was an important difference from the customs of other tribes.

Originally, every free Frank was required to provide the king with military service. In practice, though, only one individual per household was usually delegated to serve. Length of service was at the will of the ruler, but the realities of an agriculturally based life meant that most fighters confined their service to the three-month period between planting and harvest. This form of feudalism was the social structure that evolved in Western Europe — and to some degree England — by the ninth century.

Powerful as the Frankish rulers became, they could not extend their authority beyond the grave. At a time in world history when material wealth was scarce, people took any opportunity they could to wrest property away from the weak or disabled. The death of each Frankish king led to struggles among his descendents over who got what part of the kingdom. Dukes and counts scrambled to amass power and keep the peace, and that necessitated building up their own personal fighting forces. Those on the lower rungs of the economic ladder increasingly sought protection from dukes and counts in exchange for service.

Vassals & Vassalage

Certain practices became standardized. An individual who received protection from a duke or count was called a vassal. While the word originally meant slave and in modern times still carries that negative connotation, it had a more technical and positive meaning in the Middle Ages. A vassal at that time was simply a freeman who was contractually dependent on another freeman. Once the commitment for protection was made, it was considered inviolate. In return for their service — military or other — a duke or count was expected to provide his followers with "gifts." These might be gold ornaments, horses, weapons, or food and wine, as well as land. Any material property was to be returned upon death, when the commitment ended.

The seriousness of the lifetime commitment involved in vassalage required a special ceremony, called commendation. The person seeking protection knelt and placed his hands in those of his lord. The vassal then swore, in an oath of fealty, to be faithful to his overlord. The lord kissed him and raised him up in an act of homage. A symbol of the contract — a clod of earth, a stick or a piece of straw — would be given to the vassal. In exchange for protection against their enemies, vassals provided military service or other labor — agricultural, administrative or judicial — according to rank. Loyalty even beyond death could be expected. An overlord was required to avenge the murder of his vassal with the blood of the killer or with a fine collected from the killer. If the lord himself was killed, his vassals were likewise expected to exact revenge or suffer dishonor.

The only way — besides death — that the contract could be broken was if a lord struck his vassal or tried to kill him, if he seduced his wife or daughter, deprived him of his patrimony, or failed to defend him. By the ninth century, a vassal was defined exclusively as an individual who undertook military duties and came equipped with horse, lance, shield and sword. In other words, a vassal was a miles or knight.

Fiefs & Benefices

The precedent had existed in Western Europe since Roman days for large tracts of land to be leased to farmers in exchange for labor. This arrangement was also practiced by the Church, since it was not allowed to sell its land holdings. An arrangement similar to these loan agreements, known as a benefice or fief, continued among the Frankish leaders. The word fief originally meant ownership of cows. It referred to the fact that a fief holder had use of the cattle on the land he had been provided on loan. The connection between cattle and land reflects a society where

ABOVE: **An early depiction of a king distributing royal charters to his vassals. These were his lords, and all his patrimony descended through them to their followers in return for oaths of fealty.**

people had once been migratory, tending wandering flocks of livestock. Their world gradually became one in which they planted crops and worked the land, as well as herding livestock.

The need to maintain strong fighting forces in the face of civil disputes and invasions led to a joining of vassalage with benefices. By rewarding retainers with land grants that were in effect rent-free, a lord could ensure the wholehearted support of his vassals. At the bottom of the pecking order, the peasants provided the labor that enabled a lord to perform his military duties as a knight.

This system, known as fiefdom, enabled vassals to accumulate the property, wealth and power that became a foundation for knighthood. By the time of Charles "the Hammer" Martel, fiefs granted to a father began to be passed on and might stay in a family for generations or even permanently. The arrangement, although not yet truly hereditary since it had not been made into law, was confirmed through the ceremony of commendation. Ultimately, Charlemagne's grandson Charles the Bald issued a decree that any count who died while the king was away might be succeeded by his son. This law of hereditary privilege applied also to royal vassals, and their minions.

Since vassalage and fiefdom were based on the personal relationship between lord and vassal, the forms feudalism took were many. A count might serve as a vassal to a prince and a duke at the same time. The same count might divide his benefices acquired from his vassalage among his own vassals. He might also hold property on his own that was not subject to vassalage. The need for such an elaborate system stemmed from the cost of equipping and maintaining a fighting force. Feudalism was most deeply entrenched in those regions of Western Europe that fell under the control of the Franks: Germany, France, Italy and Spain. It was least evident in Norway, Denmark, Sweden, Poland and Hungary. In England, where the influence of the Roman Empire was less pervasive than in Western Europe, feudalism had a limited development, and society there remained more open to individuals who were not knights.

Horses, Swords & Body Armor

By the time Martel stemmed the Moorish tide at Poitiers in the eighth century, Frankish soldiers were carrying swords as well as shields. They also wore breast plates and were riding horses. Traditionally the Franks had fought as foot soldiers, but they soon switched to cavalry. Soldiers on horseback began carrying heavier spears, more than six and a half feet in length. Leaders might wear a helm with ear-flaps and a mail neck-guard, adapted from the style of the Roman Empire.

nofus armis
pidantia cord

Early knights also carried several knives and a francisca, which was a light throwing axe. Both a short and a longer sword would be part of a Frankish chieftain's military gear, along with gem-decorated hilts of leather and wood.

The headgear of the early Frankish warriors, called spangenhelm from the German for "buckled helmet," were likely to be designed for status more than safety. They are thought to have been adapted originally from the felt hats worn by the same nomadic tribes who set in motion the early barbarian invasions. They also bear a resemblance, though, to late Roman helmets made in the imperial arms factories of the fourth and fifth centuries. The early versions were made of three pieces, consisting of two half-skulls riveted to a central comb. Later spangenhelms were constructed in the following manner. Vertical bands of bronze were riveted to a metal brow band. The point at the top of the helm where the bands met had a plume holder, which might contain horsehair. Between the bronze bands, iron plates were riveted on the inside of the helm. These plates might be covered with bronze or silver and decorated with semi-precious stones. The entire helm, with

protective ear flaps and mail neck guards in early versions, was lined with leather. Ear flaps and neck guards were abandoned after the ninth century and then re-adopted in the 13th century.

Swords of the period were pattern-welded. The blade had a groove running down the center of both sides. The sword's core consisted of a series of iron bars welded together. The bars were made of case-hardened, twisted iron strips. Case-hardening produced a softer, malleable core with a harder outside surface, giving the blade greater flexibility through a process of quenching, or cooling, and tempering, or reheating. The finished product would be sharpened, polished and etched to bring out the twisted pattern in the bars of the weapon's core.

The reason for using such a complex process was that while iron ore was becoming more readily available, it was difficult for ironworkers to find large enough pieces of consistent purity. Because the changes in color of the iron as it was being welded were critical to the quality of the product, metalworkers often labored at night, the better to observe the color differences and control the tempering process. The skills of a good smith were highly valued. In keeping with a culture that relied more on objects than words, different metals had different meanings. Silver, for instance, was often used as an inlay on a sword because soldiers believed it had the power to protect the sword from blunting.

While bow-and-arrow weaponry existed from the time of the Bronze Age, the Franks probably did not use them. Arrowheads are often found in early Frankish graves, but no mention is made of this type of weaponry in historical records.

Early Forms of Mail Armor

Mail shirts became an increasingly valued form of protection for Frankish fighters toward the end of the first millennium. Called byrnies or — when longer — hauberks, they were made from iron wire riveted into individual rings. To create mail, four separate links were attached to each individual iron ring, and it took more than 30,000 links to make a single mail shirt. Frankish mail shirts were knee length, with a split in the front and back of the skirt for riding. The shirt was pulled on over the head through a front slit. The Frankish byrnie or hauberk usually had short sleeves, but the sleeves might extend to elbow length. A wool tunic was usually worn underneath the mail.

Just how costly military equipment and weaponry were in the time of the Carolingian Empire of the Franks is demonstrated by translating their value into livestock: a byrnie was worth 12 cows; a horse, also 12 cows; sword and scabbard, seven cows; a helm, six cows; leg armor, six cows; lance and shield, two cows.

ABOVE: **A plan showing the arrangement of land at a relatively small (150 residents) 12th-century feudal manor.**

ABOVE: **A sixth-century** *spangen-helm* **from France. Made in several parts, it had a bronze frame with riveted triangular iron plates and separate earpieces.**

Anglo-Saxon Invasions of England

While the Franks were reinforcing their control over Western Europe, the Angles, Saxons and Jutes were invading England from the sixth to the eighth centuries. They came from northern Europe and probably established themselves in much the same way that the Franks had in Western Europe: as Roman auxiliaries. In exchange for land, they agreed to protect the region from further invasions for the Roman colonists. The native Britons resisted fiercely, probably leading to a consolidation of forces among the rag-tag bands of Angles, Saxons and Jutes, identified in modern times by the umbrella term Anglo-Saxons.

The Anglo-Saxons fought with spears, their socket-heads sometimes inlaid with silver, copper or bronze. Unlike the Franks, though, they didn't use barbed spears. Swords held a special, even magical place in Anglo-Saxon society. In poems of the time they were called heirlooms, a term that in modern parlance is more apt to mean family jewels. Warriors believed that a sword retained the luck, courage and skills of its previous owners, so a sword was cherished and passed on from generation to generation. The mythology that grew up around swords claimed that they were made by giants such as the legendary ironsmith Weland. Some swords had a small ring attached at the pommel, which may have been used for oath-taking. Or it could have served simply to symbolize the close relationship between a king and his retainer. Anglo-Saxon sword blades were very similar to those of the Franks and were likely to be imported. Hilts, however, were probably local, allowing them to be changed according to fashion.

Early Anglo-Saxon shields were round like those of the Franks, with an iron boss and handle, and occasionally a metal rim. They were usually made of linden wood and covered with bull's hide. A warrior put his hand through a leather strap or brace, which fixed the device firmly onto his forearm, and then into the metal grip in the center on the inside. A second strap probably allowed the owner to hang up the shield or sling it on his back. The Anglo-Saxons did not initially have body armor. Some armor was found, however, at Sutton Hoo, one of the more famous Anglo-Saxon grave sites, where an entire ship was buried. The Sutton Hoo armor had butted rings, which meant it was probably meant to be ceremonial and was not designed for fighting, since the metal rings had not been riveted shut.

The Role of the Church

While the continued threat of invasion spurred the Frankish tribes in Western Europe to develop feudalism as a means of social organization, knighthood did not really come into being until the Frankish leaders joined forces with the Roman

Catholic Church. The Pope, as Bishop of Rome, had long claimed to be the spiritual leader of all Christians in the Western world. The Church also wanted to play a political role in Western Europe, and Charles Martel saw a benefit in aligning himself with the Church. As Mayor of the Palace for the Merovingian royalty, he gave his support to the missionary work in Frankish territories of the English monk St. Boniface. When Pepin the Short succeeded his father, he continued that support of the Church and built on it.

Martel was responsible for starting a new dynasty of Frankish rulers that followed the Merovingians. They were named the Carolingians after their greatest leader Charlemagne. The Carolingian Empire, which spanned the period of 751 A.D. to 987 A.D., combined elements of both Roman and Germanic traditions. From the Germanic tribes came the reliance on personal relationships as a means of social and military organization. From the Roman Empire came the adoption of institutional and administrative structures, including the Carolingian alliance with the Roman Catholic Church.

BELOW: Medieval swords and daggers. The knight regarded his sword not only as a weapon but also as a symbol of his status and power.

After Martel's death in 741 A.D., the Frankish territories were divided between his two sons, Pepin the Short and Carloman. Carloman retired to religious life, after which Pepin became sole leader, in fact if not in title. Led by St. Boniface, who came to be known as the Apostle of the Germans, Anglo-Saxon missionaries were working to convert the German tribes east of the Rhine. Pepin the Short supported their campaign, although not for religious reasons alone. The Germanic tribes that the missionaries were trying to convert — Thuringians, Bavarians, Saxons and Frisians — all shared borders with the Franks and therefore were potential military threats.

Eventually Pope Zacharias plotted with Pepin to remove the ruling Merovingian ruler and have Pepin declared king. In exchange, Pepin agreed to defend Rome from Lombard invasion. Winning back Ravenna and a number of other Italian cities, he gave the Church the territories he won in those campaigns. These terri-

ABOVE: **The crown first used at the coronation of Charlemagne in 800 A.D., and then for all the rulers of the Carolingian and Holy Roman Empires.**

BELOW: **A Danish or Jute shirt of mail from before 450 A.D. Such a shirt might contain as many as 30,000 links.**

tories provided the basis for the political entity known as the Papal States. The Church's blessing provided a crucial spiritual reinforcement to knighthood. When Pope Leo III crowned Martel's grandson Charlemagne as Emperor on Christmas Day, 800 A.D., the last piece fell into place. A new era was about to begin.

The Moorish Threat

Barbarian Germanic tribes were not the only invading force to menace Western Europe. The threat from the south came from Islamic converts, or Moors, who left the Arabian peninsula, moved west across northern Africa and invaded what is now Spain. In 613 A.D., the great Islamic prophet Mohammed had begun to call for the submission of all Arab people to one God under Islam. His uniting of the Arab people and formation of a theocracy led to development of a powerful Islamic fighting force, driven by religious zeal. Moors who died in battle against infidels, which included Christians and barbarians alike, looked forward to eternal paradise.

When Mohammed died in 632 A.D., his father-in-law Abu Bakr appointed himself Caliph, or successor, and began the waves of invasion. Equipped with Arabian horses — known for their speed and endurance — the Moors moved in quickly, using the element of surprise. Fighting with swords, lances and bows and arrows but no body armor, they avoided traveling with cumbersome baggage trains that could slow them down. Used to a harsh desert climate, they and their horses and camels could go for great distances without food and water.

Unlike the Germanic tribes invading from the north and east, the Moors did not assimilate into the culture of the Western European territories they invaded. Once they subdued a region, they levied taxes but remained aloof from populations they considered to consist of infidels. They overran the Spanish peninsula by 711 A.D. Their main objective, however, was Constantinople, probably the richest city in the world during the Middle Ages. Capitol of the Byzantine Empire then and now part of Turkey, Constantinople was beseiged repeatedly by the Moors, beginning in 655 A.D. The Byzantine Emperor Leo staved off Moorish attack decisively in 717 A.D. with the help of Greek fire, a highly flammable combination of naphtha and sulphur quicklime.

From Spain, the Moors entered Frankish territory: Aquitaine in 712 A.D., Narbonne in 719 A.D., Toulouse in 722 A.D. At the time, the Merovingian rulers of the Franks were in decline, and the

ABOVE: **An undated woodcut shows Charles Martel halting the Moorish advances at the Battle of Poitiers in 732 A.D.**

region was subject to constant turmoil. The Moors initially were stopped by Eudo, a Frankish duke from Aquitaine, but they returned in 725 A.D. to occupy Nimes and Carcassonne. In a reflection of the political anarchy that predominated, Eudo declared independence from Frankish rule, but then was subdued and "repatriated" by Charles "the Hammer" Martel. After forming an alliance with a Moorish chieftain and marrying his daughter, Eudo found his new Moorish ally quashed in a political struggle by the Moorish governor of Spain. The Spanish governor abducted Eudo's wife and sent her to the Caliph's harem in Damascus. After razing Bordeaux, the Moorish governor headed toward Tours but was stopped by Charles Martel in the now-famous Battle of Poitiers in 732 A.D.

While the Moors attacked on horseback in the fight outside Tours, the Frankish forces fought on foot, repelling one mounted charge after another. When the battle ended at nightfall, the Moorish leader was killed and his forces routed. The defeat was temporary, though, and Moorish forces returned in 735 A.D. and 759 A.D. As powerful an effect as the invasions of the Germanic tribes had, those tribes did not change the prevailing cultural conditions of Western Europe. That was not the case with the Moors. Where they settled, the Moors succeeded in cutting off Western Europe from the Mediterranean and its ties with the Byzantine Empire. Their most important contribution of all to Medieval knighthood, though, was probably their use of horses in warfare.

The First Knight: Charlemagne

I f any one warrior deserves to be called the first Medieval knight, it is Charlemagne. His father, Pepin the Short, had been an active military leader, but Charlemagne brought order to the Frankish kingdom. He marched across Western Europe with a retinue of knights, ousting invaders and establishing peace. It took him a lifetime, but his leadership brought discipline to the ranks of knighthood and inspired the loyalty of individual knights. In many ways, he shaped the nature of knighthood and Medieval warfare.

The Church played an important role in legitimating Charlemagne's rule. After his father's death in 768 A.D., Charlemagne divided up the entire Frankish kingdom with his younger brother Carloman. He was 26 years old. Two years later, Carloman's death led to a war of succession. Desiderius, the King of the Lombards, entered the fray on the side of Carloman's young sons, but Pope Adrian I favored the other side. Charlemagne aligned himself with the pope against his nephews. When the Lombard ruler took refuge in Pavia — now part of Italy — after the Carolingians invaded, Charlemagne blockaded the city for nine months through the winter of 773-774 A.D. When Desiderius conceded, he assumed the iron crown of Lombardy. Later when a new pope, Leo III, was threatened with deposition, Charlemagne marched to Rome to support him. His reward was to be crowned as Emperor of the Holy Roman Empire on Christmas Day in 800 A.D.

Charlemagne — also known as Charles the Great — inherited a vast expanse of territory. His motives for increasing it further were not much different from those of the barbarian hordes who still threatened Western Europe: plunder and increased land holdings. The difference was that once he was crowned Emperor, Charlemagne's expansion was legitimated by the Church. His skill as a military strategist is also an important part of his legacy to the modern world as the first true knight.

Saxony — the region northeast of Frankish territory in what is now

BELOW: **A Carolingian silver cup with an interlace design and bird motif. Found in Denmark, it was probably taken there by Vikings.**

OPPOSITE: **Detail of a miniature depicting Charlemagne's Frankish knights and infantry as they fought across Western Europe.**

northern Germany — was Charlemagne's main focus during most of his military career. The area can be characterized geographically as swampy, difficult terrain. Saxony was a military challenge, and it took Charlemagne some 33 years of off-and-on fighting against different groups of Saxons to subdue the region. He used extreme measures: slaughtering the natives, forcing their religious conversion and exiling thousands of them to the Frankish kingdom. In 782 A.D., he beheaded 4,500 Saxons in one day for burning churches and killing missionaries.

Sieges & Skirmishes

When focusing his energies on the subduing of Saxony — now northern Germany — Charlemagne waged his campaigns in a manner typical of the times. His military actions against the Saxons began as border disputes and consisted mostly of intermittent skirmishes and sieges of fortified towns. Conventional battles, sometimes using multiple columns, might be fought — the Franks were defeated by the Saxons in the Suntel Mountains during such a battle in 782 A.D. — but these battles were rarely decisive or permanent. The royal records kept by Charlemagne spend relatively little time detailing them. Raids for the purpose of plundering — an important source of income for knights — were more common than staged battles.

An illustration of the variable nature of conquest during this early period of knighthood is the Saxon campaign of 776-777 A.D. Charlemagne defeated the southern Saxons at Lippespringe on the Ems River. As soon as his armies with-

drew, the Saxons rebelled again, rejecting their conversion to Christianity. Before he was able to defeat the Saxon chief Widukind and have him baptized, Charlemagne spent a winter in Saxony, ravaging the countryside. He built forts there and garrisoned his soldiers in them. Since fighting usually stopped during the winter months, this strategy proved to be a successful innovation. In 784 A.D. he set up his court at Eresburg in Saxony for Christmas and Easter, keeping up the pressure all winter long.

One of Charlemagne's military strengths was his ability to fight in a variety of locations. His resources were great enough that he could field several well-equipped armies of knights in the same year, sometimes using converging columns against his adversaries. Careful logistical organization allowed Charlemagne to maintain supply trains that replenished his armies on a regular basis. This method replaced the foraging that his knights had depended on previously. Foraging did not provide a reliable supply source, and when it was unsuccessful, fighters invariably dispersed. Foraging also antagonized people in friendly areas and exposed smaller bands of knights to attack in hostile territory.

ABOVE: **An undated woodcut depicting Charlemagne inflicting baptism upon the Saxons.**

From Saxony to Lombard & Spain

Estimates of the knights raised by Charlemagne's royal vassals reach as high as 35,000. He used his armies to strike in a variety of places in addition to Saxony. In 773 and 774 A.D., his forces fought in Lombardy — what is now northern Italy — and they were active in northern Spain in 778 A.D. The Battle of Roncevalles in 778 A.D. was an early example of guerrilla warfare. Charlemagne was leaving Spain after a series of campaigns against the Moors. He had been defeated at Saragossa. As his knights made their way through the Roncevalles Pass in the Pyrénées Mountains, Christian Basques ambushed the baggage train and its escort, vanishing into the woods once reinforcements from the main army reached the scene. The Franks complained bitterly about the rout, as recorded in the Revised Annals of the Kingdom of the Franks: ". . . they (Charlemagne's forces) were rendered their inferiors by the steepness of the terrain and the character of the battle, which was not fought fairly." The rout was immortalized in the epic poem, *The Song of Roland* where it was transformed into a mythic struggle against the Moors. Later on, Charlemagne's forces did wrest the Spanish border from Pamplona to Barcelona — it was known as the Spanish March — from Moorish control.

Charlemagne's move against the Avars in Bavaria — now part of Germany — in 790-791 A.D. provides a good illustration of how he arranged his forces to outwit the enemy. He and his knights had first fought against these Hun nomads,

ABOVE: **Pepin the Short, the first Carolingian king of the Franks and the father of Charlemagne.**

BELOW: **Frankish infantry and cavalry of the Carolingian Empire, from a page of the Golden Psalter.**

who had enslaved the Slav tribes in the Danube River region, in 787 A.D. in Bavaria. The origin of the word "slave" comes from the Avars' oppression of Slav natives. Charlemagne concentrated his forces at Regensburg and marshalled an army from Lombardy for rear action through Pannonia in what is now Hungary, Austria and Yugoslavia. A force of Frank, Saxon, Thuringian and Frisian knights massed north of the Danube River and helped the main army outflank the Avars. It took 15 oxen-driven wagons to carry the Avar treasure back to Charlemagne's court. By the end of the eighth century, Charlemagne began delegating leadership to dukes and subordinates like Eric of Friuli. He left his son Pippin in charge when he went to Rome to be crowned emperor, after which he retired for all intents and purposes. Subsequent Carolingian campaigns against the Slavs and the Moors, as well as in Italy and on the Mediterranean were fought by his subordinates and his sons.

The Role of Horses

Carolingian military successes, starting with those of Charlemagne's grandfather Charles Martel, can be traced to the increased use of horses — one of the critical components of knighthood — in warfare. An early Frankish campaign against the Saxons in 626 A.D. provides the first record of a decisive use of cavalry. Pepin the Short postponed the annual spring assembly of forces in 755 A.D. because there was not yet enough grass for the horses. It is not accurate, however, to credit the Franks early in their campaigns with use of the stirrup — so crucial to the development of cavalry tactics.

Used in Asia during the fifth century, the stirrup was employed by the Moors in the seventh century and appeared in Europe on Avar and Lombard warriors' horses in the eighth century. They were not used extensively by the Franks until the end of the eighth century. The mobility gained by the use of cavalry was nevertheless the important element of the Frankish knights' success, along with the size of Charlemagne's armies. Charlemagne's knights still fought primarily with swords and lances as striking and throwing weapons, not with lances that were couched, or tucked under the arm. The stability provided by stirrups permitted couched lances. In addition to offering mobility to Frankish mounted troops, horses remained important to them simply as a means of support for soldiers and equipment. The records of Charlemagne's summoning of Lombard troops in 786 A.D. suggest that these knights were to serve on horseback. By 806 A.D., a letter from Charlemagne to Abbot Fulrad calling him to serve implies that all the bishop's men were to be mounted. By the time Charlemagne's grandson Charles the Bald was ruling in the second half of the ninth century, the Frankish army was clearly a mounted one, and in 891 A.D. the Annals of the Kingdom of the Franks stated that Frankish knights no longer even knew how to fight on foot.

Military Organization

The size of the Frankish armies and its geographic range of operation necessitated tight organization. Knights had to provide their own supplies, since they were not issued by the king. Charlemagne required that each knight bring with him a three-month supply of food, along with a six-month supply of weaponry and clothing. The Frankish leader even went so far as to define the three-month period as starting at the frontier, so that knights had to provide additional supplies for use until they reached designated locations. Provisions might include flour, wine, pork, mills for corn, adzes, axes, augers, slings for siege engines and rocks for ammunition. Carts were expected to hold 12 bushels of corn or 12 barrels of wine. Their leather covers, when laced and stuffed with hay, doubled as pontoons for crossing rivers.

Entire herds of cattle traveled with the soldiers. Bridges were maintained in Frankish territory, and new ones were built in Saxony for the campaigns there, with forts to protect them. Supplies were shipped down the Danube when appropriate. The Franks used a portable bridge in the 792 A.D. campaign against the Avars, and the troops had collapsible boats for crossing the Ebro River during the Spanish campaign. To improve troop communications between the forces fighting in Saxony and Hungary, Charlemagne even tried — although unsuccessfully — to build a canal linking the Rhine and Danube rivers. Such careful organization — the hallmark of the first knight — no doubt contributed in important ways to Charlemagne's eventual defeat of the Saxons.

Each year, Charlemagne usually called together his soldiers around Easter. These assemblies served as a muster for the Frankish armies and were often followed by military operations. When general campaigns were not underway,

ABOVE: **Charles II or Charles the Bald, King of the West Franks and Emperor of the West from 875, presided over an army in which mounted knights were dominant.**

Charlemagne might use smaller mobile units of several hundred men, called scarae, for minor skirmishes. The knights making up the scarae were likely to be taken from the Emperor's royal escort.

Charlemagne's 791 A.D. campaign against the Avars shows the role of the assembly in his military organization. Gathering his army in Regensburg on the Danube River, he held an assembly there in May and won the assembly's approval for the campaign. By September his forces reached the Enns River on the border of Pannonia and spent three days in prayer. A second invasion, planned for 792 A.D., never took place because of internal dissension, lack of horses and famine. These elements of life were as much the enemies of Medieval knights as other warriors proved to be.

Military Equipment

An accomplished administrator, Charlemagne established regulations for the type of military equipment each soldier, no matter what his rank, was required to have. In 792-793 A.D., he issued requirements calling for all his knights to have horses, lances, shields and both long and short swords. By 802-803 A.D., knights were also to provide themselves with body armor. As Christianity spread, the barbarian custom of burying a knight with his arms began to disappear, so less is known about the kind of armor Carolingian knights wore. Illuminated manuscripts show them wearing Roman-style armor — cuirasses or chest armor — but such illustrations cannot be relied on as necessarily accurate. Part of the equipment found in the Sutton Hoo funereal ship of the Saxons in England consists of gold-hinged clasps. These might have been part of a leather cuirass, indicating that such a style was still being worn there.

In an edict issued in 805 A.D., Charlemagne ordered every soldier with 300 acres of land to wear a byrnie or mail tunic. He also stipulated that knights who possessed byrnies but did not bring their armor with them when summoned could be penalized by losing their benefice — or land and equipment loan — including the byrnie. Charlemagne's own armor was described by the Monk of St. Gall:

> *Then appeared the Iron King, crowned with his iron helm, with iron sleeves and his breast protected by a mail shirt . . . . His thighs were covered with mail, though other men preferred to leave theirs unprotected . . . . His legs and those of most of his army were protected by iron greaves.*

In addition to mail, another form of body armor known to be in use during this period of knighthood consisted of a scale tunic, in which small pieces of metal or horn were riveted onto fabric or leather. Chausses or leg protection — called

greaves or jambes when protecting only below the knee — and arm protections were probably not yet common. A description of Charlemagne fighting at Pavia, the capital of Lombardy, in 773 A.D., says he and his knights wore greaves or shin armor. The account was written long after his death, however, and may not be accurate. Greaves were likely to have been made of long strips of metal or whalebone. Charlemagne was also said to wear a form of thigh armor made out of scales. No Frankish helmets survive from the time of Charlemagne.

Carolingian Swords & Weaponry

Frankish swords of the Carolingian period had slightly larger blades than those of earlier periods. They were much coveted by the invading Moors, reflecting the quality of workmanship. By the 10th century, the blades tapered from hilt to point, shifting the center of balance toward the hilt and making it lighter to wield. It was

well-suited for hacking, its primary use at the time, but also for thrusting. In addition to pattern-welded swords, Carolingian knights began using swords made entirely of a strong steel by the 10th century. In many cases, these swords carry the name of their makers in large iron letters just below the hilt. Carolingian spears had long, leaf-shaped blades with lugs on the socket to keep the point from becoming too deeply imbedded. The shaft might be bound with leather thongs to improve the grip.

The prevailing style of shield at the end of the ninth century was round and convex. By the end of the 10th century, it remained rounded on top, but was lengthened into a point on the bottom to protect the vulnerable left leg of a knight on horseback. Some illuminated manuscripts show Carolingian knights wearing wide-brimmed, Roman-style crested helms. Others show them with either hemispherical or conical helms.

Counts were delegated the task of checking to be sure their knights had shields, spears, bows and twelve arrows each. Even attendants and carters — or wagoneers — were required to carry bows instead of staves or wooden sticks. The export of armor and equipment was prohibited throughout Charlemagne's reign. Such regulations helped improve the general standard of arming. The Frankish ruler also worked to improve discipline, forbidding drunkenness, setting a hefty fine for failure to respond to a muster, and establishing death and confiscation of all property as the penalties for desertion.

Under Charlemagne, knights had, in effect, become professional soldiers rather than just seasonal volunteers. Only a small portion of the forces available would be called up for a specific campaign, which helped distribute military duty across the population. A count was required to bring with him all his vassals who had benefices. He was, however, allowed to leave two behind to guard his wife and two more to protect each of his territories. A duke might be put in charge of several counts, with special responsibilities delegated for guard duty. Exemptions did not apply to religious figures like bishops and abbots, although they could leave two vassals behind as guards. Any royal vassal serving at court, though exempted from military service himself, was still required to send his vassals to the Frankish army under the leadership of the count whose district they came from.

The Introduction of Selective Service

Since Charlemagne needed many well-equipped warriors, he introduced what was, in effect, selective service for the less affluent knights. An edict of 806 A.D. reflects the levying process for Charlemagne's armies. Five Saxons were required to equip a

ABOVE: **Charlemagne dictating to Alcuin, the English scholar whom he had invited to Aachen to establish a system of education.**

ABOVE: **A drawing of a Carolingian king, probably meant to be Charlemagne. Little is known of Charlemagne's actual appearance, though it is recorded that he wore the simple Frankish clothing of his forebears.**

sixth for campaigning in Spain; two were to equip a third for fighting in Bohemia and all forces were to fight against the nearby Sorbs. This system enabled Charlemagne to mount operations simultaneously at the Ebro, the Elbe, the Danube rivers and on the Breton borders without completely depleting the manpower for other necessary tasks in home territory. When the Lombards moved to stop the Carolingian army by blocking passes through the Alps, Charlemagne outflanked them by using two separate columns of soldiers. He used a similar strategy in Spain in 778 A.D., in Bavaria in 787 A.D. and in Pannonia in 791 A.D. A pincer movement was used against the Saxons in 792 A.D.

The hit-and-run raids of the early Frankish tribes were replaced by Charlemagne with a military structure that allowed for more sustained conquest. Winning a battle remained less important than establishing a permanent garrison, capturing an enemy fortress or outlasting the opponent in the field. The profit motive continued to be the primary incentive for fighting: slaves, booty, and new territories enriched the pockets of the dukes, counts and their vassals, as well as the king. Avar plunder, for example, was sent to Charlemagne by Eric of Friuli in 796 A.D., and the king then distributed it among his followers.

By the end of the eighth century, Charlemagne had already begun delegating leadership to dukes and subordinates like Eric of Friuli — the region straddling what is now Italy and Yugoslavia. The Frankish king left his son Pippin in charge when he went to Rome to be crowned emperor, after which he retired from active combat. The later Frankish campaigns against the Slavs and Moors, as well as in Italy and the Mediterranean, were fought by his sons or his subordinates.

Consolidation of the Frankish Empire

By 800 A.D. Charlemagne's strategy shifted from expansion to defense of existing territories. The need for more fighting men had led Charlemagne to extend his military drafts to include poorer freemen. Because the campaigns against the Danes and the Moors did not result in much booty, though, the emperor found it hard to muster large forces from this segment of the population. He eventually reduced the fine for not answering a muster in the case of his poorer subjects. By the early ninth century, he stipulated that only those who possessed six pounds of gold, goods and livestock had to pay the full fine, and that was as long as their women and children were not deprived of their garments. He also ordered the confiscation of royal benefices from any who refused to serve.

Charlemagne's conquests placed the Frankish knights at center stage in the arena of Western Europe. He brought under Frankish control most of what is now

France, western Germany, northern and central Italy, Belgium, Holland, Luxem-burg, Switzerland, Austria and northern Spain. His coronation as Emperor of the Holy Roman Empire meant, in addition to the alliance with the Roman Catholic Church, that the Byzantine Empire no longer held sway in Western Europe. In effect, Charlemagne created a unified entity out of the many warring territories in Western Europe. The large numbers of knights required by his armies hastened the spread of feudalism, since the expense of equipping oneself as a knight inevit-ably led to a dependence on those who had more wealth.

By 847 A.D., Charlemagne's grandson Charles the Bald had ordered all of his subjects to choose a lord — the king or one of his vassals — for protection. Just as the earlier Merovingian rulers had maintained their power by distributing land among their followers, Charlemagne reinforced his authority by giving newly acquired territory to his vassals in the form of benefices. The strongest base of his support lay in Austrasia, the northeastern section of the Frankish kingdom, and as a result, most of his benefices went to Austrasian lords. They in turn made vassals out their followers. The problem, as had been the case in earlier Merov-ingian times, was in maintaining control over what amounted to a pyramid struc-ture. Land holdings of the Church and those of royal vassals provided only a partial counterbalance to the growing power of the counts who acted as Charlemagne's

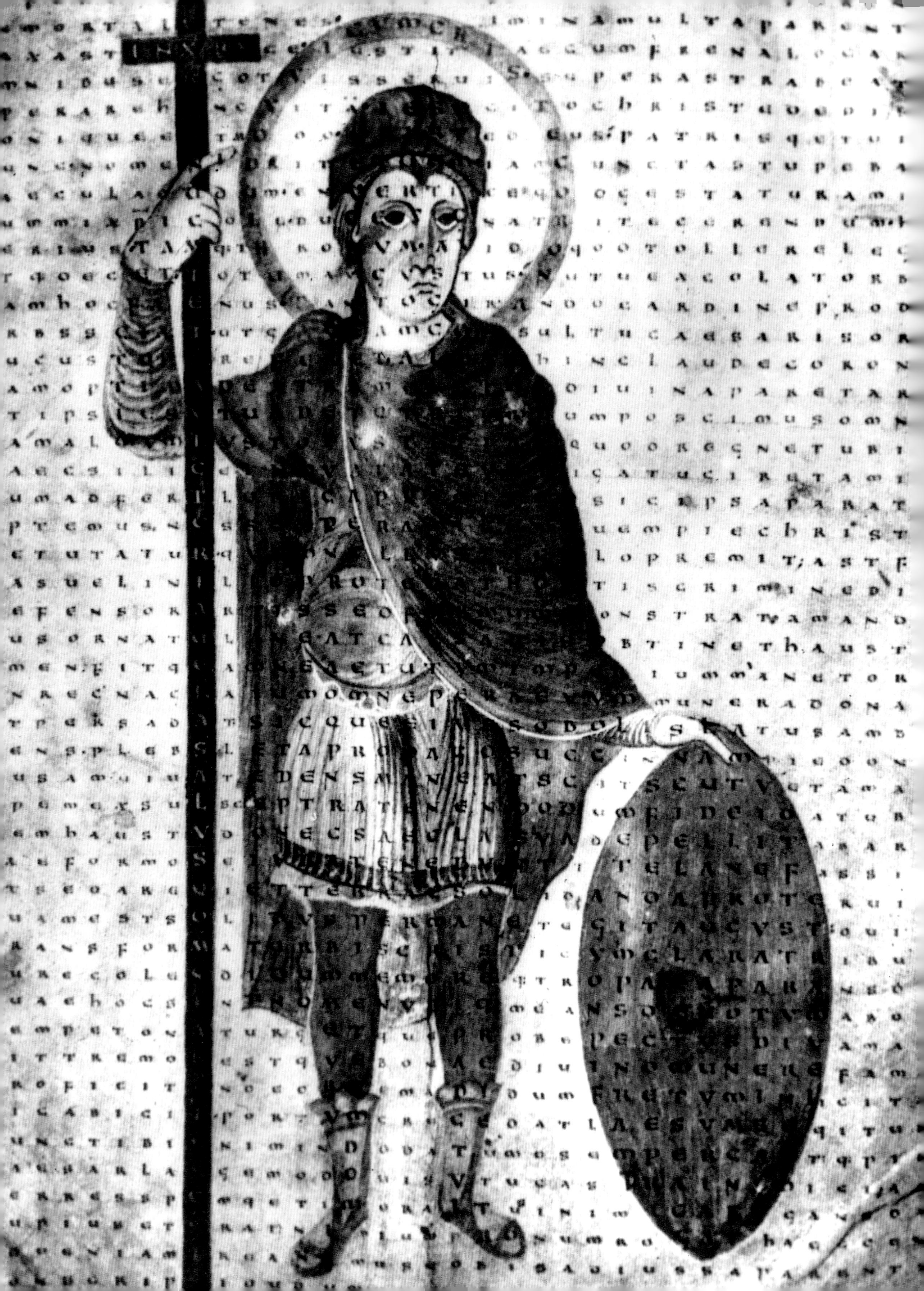

local administrators, since the former reported directly to Charlemagne and were not subject to jurisdiction by the counts.

The instability of the system may be reflected by the loyalty oath Charlemagne commanded all his royal vassals, bishops, abbots and counts to take in 792-793 A.D. The oath was to be administered by royal envoys, and the counts were required to give it in turn to the common people under their control. By the time of Charlemagne's death in 814 A.D., a vassal's greatest loyalty had transferred from his ruler to his local lord. One of the implications for knighthood of that change had to do with the understanding that vassals did not have to serve their lord if he was fighting against the king. This unwritten regulation began to be ignored. Once vassalage became hereditary, rulers had little direct control over their officers.

The End of the First Knight's Reign

Charlemagne's success in building a stable, unified kingdom out of Western Europe started to dissipate even before his death. Viking invaders took immediate advantage of Frankish political instability, and the Vikings' style of warfare was to have an important impact on knighthood. Charlemagne tried to ensure succession for his only surviving son, Louis the Pious, by crowning him king of Aquitaine in 781 A.D. and then by naming him co-emperor in 813 A.D. When the great Frankish knight died in 814 A.D., his son Louis ascended to the throne. Dissension began after Louis began to favor his son Charles, the product of a second marriage, over the three sons from his first marriage.

In the 843 A.D. Treaty of Verdun, Louis began by making his eldest son Lothair I — from his first marriage — co-emperor. He turned Aquitaine and Bavaria over to Pepin I and Louis the German, his other two sons from his first marriage. Louis next tried to take back some of the powers granted to Lothair and give them to Charles — the product of his second marriage. Lothair allied himself with his brother Pepin to retaliate, and the two of them forced their father out of power. It was just the first of a series of political reversals that weakened the Frankish kingdom, leaving it vulnerable to invasion. The tribes from the north — the Vikings — were quick to take advantage.

Invaders from the North

The Vikings came primarily from Sweden, Norway and Denmark. They were fishermen, farmers and sailors who had been active as traders since Roman times. No satisfactory explanation has ever been found for what made them turn to *i viking* — the term means sea-roving or piracy — since they left no written records

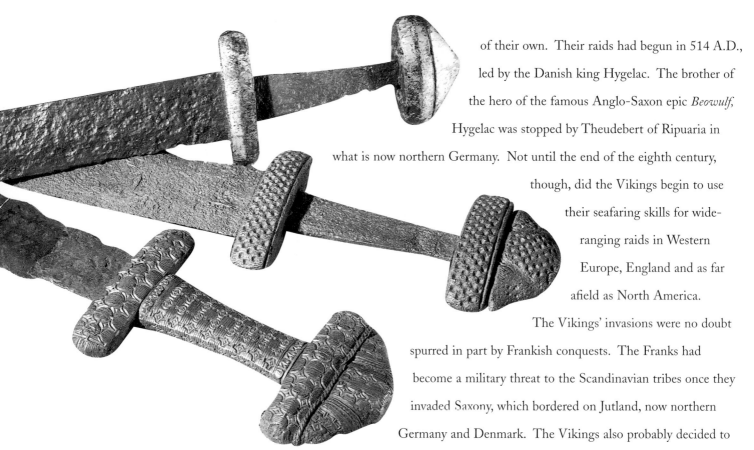

of their own. Their raids had begun in 514 A.D., led by the Danish king Hygelac. The brother of the hero of the famous Anglo-Saxon epic *Beowulf*, Hygelac was stopped by Theudebert of Ripuaria in what is now northern Germany. Not until the end of the eighth century, though, did the Vikings begin to use their seafaring skills for wide-ranging raids in Western Europe, England and as far afield as North America.

The Vikings' invasions were no doubt spurred in part by Frankish conquests. The Franks had become a military threat to the Scandinavian tribes once they invaded Saxony, which bordered on Jutland, now northern Germany and Denmark. The Vikings also probably decided to leave their own countries because of overpopulation. Polygamous societies, they produced large families with many offspring.

Their skills as sailors may have made the most important contribution of all to this period of knighthood. The introduction of the sail at the beginning of the eighth century increased the range of their raids. A Viking boat from the fourth century A.D. found in Denmark was designed solely for rowing, with low sides, no deck and places for 14 pairs of oarsmen. By the eighth century, Viking ships, longer and deeper hulled, were more easily capable of navigating the North Sea.

The Vikings, also called Norsemen, had little in the way of armor and weaponry, relying on trading or military conquests for helmets and byrnies when they could get them. By the ninth century, they had adopted the matériel of their rivals, wearing Frankish-style byrnies and carrying shields similar to those used by the Franks. They carried short, double-bladed swords with no cross-grip and small hand-grips. Their spears were Frankish in appearance. Viking axes were heavy weapons, requiring both hands to swing, and had long wooden shafts. The Vikings were accomplished archers, unrivalled by any warriors of the era except the Moors.

By 834 A.D., the Vikings began a relentless assault on the Frankish coast, from Frisia — now the Netherlands — to Gironde — now southwest France. They razed Amiens, Paris and Orleans, next entering Spain, Morocco and parts of Italy. These raiders from the North had the advantage, since they could appear suddenly anywhere along the coast or at the mouth of a river, before the Franks had time to marshal their forces. By the time Charlemagne's ancestor Charles III, also known as

TOP: **Hilts of Viking swords. By the end of the ninth century, Scandinavia had become renowned for the fine blades it manufactured.**

ABOVE: **In a surprise raid, a Viking fleet enters the Humber estuary of northeastern England.**

Charles the Fat, was emperor, Frankish politics depended on negotiation more than fighting. In 886 A.D., Charles ransomed Paris rather than engage the Norsemen in battle. He was dethroned shortly afterward.

Viking Assaults on England & Ireland

England and Ireland, as well as the Frankish kingdom, were targets of Viking raids. Political unrest and infighting made all three of these regions vulnerable. Charlemagne said to his knights about the Vikings, "I do not fear that these worthless scamps will do any harm to me. No, I am sad at heart thinking that while I live they dare to intrude upon this shore, and I am torn by a great sorrow foreseeing what evil they will do to my descendents."

The Norwegians arrived in the British Isles from the north. After a brief raid on Dorset, England, in 787 A.D., they attacked Ireland, which had escaped earlier barbarian invasion, in 795 A.D. By 853 A.D., King Olaf of Norway had established himself in Dublin, Ireland, and there were Viking colonies in Wexford, Waterford and Limerick. They stayed until the Norman conquest in the 11th century. The Danes used a southerly route, attacking England, sections of the Frankish territories that now make up the Netherlands and Belgium, and even reaching as far as Sicily.

In the initial stages, the Vikings arrived offshore in their ships, plundered the countryside and returned home. In time, though, they came to settle, even building their own cities in the case of Ireland. The appearance of their fleets on the shores of England, Ireland and the Frankish territories instilled terror in the local populace. Boats, each carrying up to 40 soldiers, could penetrate deeply into these regions by sailing up rivers and estuaries. Once disembarked, they rustled every available horse and moved rapidly inland.

Monasteries and churches were particularly vulnerable. King Egbert of Wessex repulsed the Danes in 838 A.D., but they returned in 840 A.D. to pillage London, Lincolnshire and Northumbria. It took King Alfred of Wessex to stop the onslaught.

Recognizing the importance of sea power strategy — neglected by the Franks

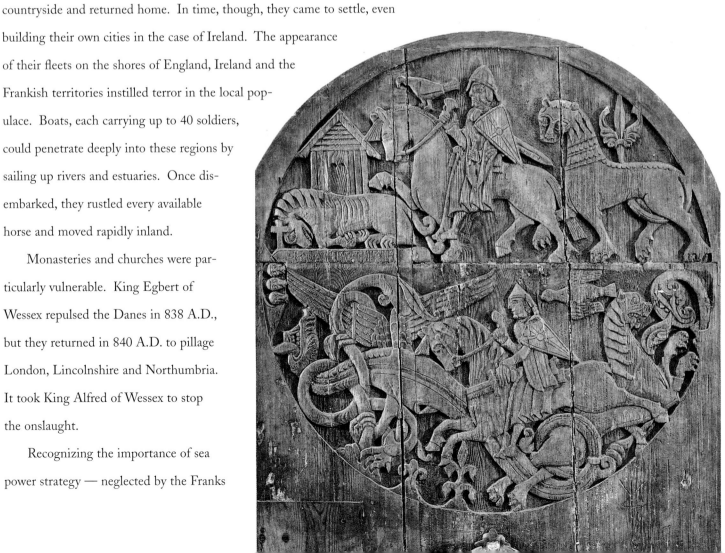

— Alfred bought time by negotiating with the Danes by agreeing to pay them tributes. He ordered construction of a fleet of long boats, although his forces could not match Viking nautical experience. Alfred also built fortifications. After five years of paying tribute, he was ready to fight. In 878 A.D. he defeated the Danish leader Guthrum at Edington. Guthrum was baptized, and an agreement was worked out to limit the degree of Danish settlement. When the Danes invaded again in 892-896 A.D., they were unsuccessful. Alfred's victory bears significance well beyond the shores of England, since a Viking enclave there would have put all of Western Europe at risk.

The threat from the North led to important military developments in the ninth century. Volunteer forces of foot soldiers were unable to stop the Vikings, and the professional skills of a retinue of knights — well armed and on horseback — became increasingly valuable. Knights on horseback were able to match the speed of the Vikings for the first time.

The Magyars

With the Frankish leadership in disarray, the tribes of Saxony, Bavaria, Swabia, Franconia and Lorraine — covering what is now western Germany and France — banded together and elected their own leader in 919 A.D. Duke Henry of Saxony served as the first King of what is now Germany. His main concern was the Magyars, who had first invaded eastern Bavaria — now Austria — in 862 A.D. Like the

LEFT: **Arpad, chief of the Magyars, led his nomadic people westward late in the ninth century. Their advance was finally stopped by Otto I at Augsburg in 955 A.D.**

Vikings, they regularly swooped in on horses, collected booty and left. Their preferred strategy was to surround their opponents, who were less mobile, and barrage them with arrows from all sides until they broke ranks from exhaustion, casualties and frustration.

Conciliation was the first tactic that Henry tried. In 924 A.D., he agreed to give tribute, but then he followed the path of Alfred the Great in England and began to build up his forces. Fortifications were built along the German borders, leading to the establishment of such cities as Nordhausen, Merseburg, Quedlinburg and Goslar. The task of constructing these fortifications was delegated to the local populace, with help from prisoners. When the Magyars attacked Thuringia in 933 A.D., Henry was ready. He turned them back at the Unstrut River in central Germany.

After Henry's death, the Magyars resumed their invasions. Henry's son and successor, Otto I, confronted the Magyars with 7,000 mounted knights at Augsburg on the Lech River in 955 A.D. The battle was hard fought, with many casualties on both sides. One detachment of Swabian knights was hit from the rear by the Magyars and slaughtered, until Conrad, Duke of Franconia east of the Rhine River, arrived with reinforcements. Duke Conrad was killed when he removed his helmet to get some air. After two days of fighting, Otto finally routed the Magyars, who were riding smaller horses than the Germans and fought without armor, although they compensated by using bows and arrows. The Germans captured several Magyar leaders and hanged them, ending the Magyar threat to Western Europe.

The establishment of knighthood by Charlemagne and his Carolingian heirs during the ninth century changed the face of Western society. From the Frankish kingdom, knighthood spread throughout Europe and England. The new method of keeping order was a success, and Charlemagne's strategy of building fortifications led to the development of one of knighthood's hallmarks, the castle.

From Fortification to Castle

A key component of Charlemagne's military organization was fortification. As the first knight advanced against each new tribe or province, he constructed frontier outposts, called burgs, that were heavily fortified and usually made of wood. Once these fortifications went up, he connected them with roads so that they could maintain contact both with other outposts and the seat of operations. Charlemagne's fortified outposts were kept stocked with supplies so that they could serve as bases for the Frankish army as it conducted its maneuvers.

The capturing of enemy fortifications served as an equally important strategy of knightly warfare. Siegecraft — the tactics and equipment used in breaching a stronghold — became highly developed. Fortification had been an adjunct to warfare since long before the time of Charlemagne, but up until the Middle Ages it had a strictly military function. Out of military fortifications evolved the castle, made first of wood and eventually of stone. In addition to serving as a military stronghold, the Medieval castle also served as a residence, secular or religious. In the case of kings, it also operated as the seat of government. Called the most closely integrated form of military and civilian life the world has ever seen, the castle is one of the hallmarks of knighthood and Medieval life in general.

After Charlemagne's death, the continued invasions of Frankish territory by Vikings and Magyars stimulated the construction of more fortifications. Some of these new fortifications protected rural populations; others were built to defend commercial centers. With central authority eroded by the internecine squabbles among Charlemagne's heirs, permanent military forces were built up by individual dukes and lords. These private armies were garrisoned in fortifications. Initially, fortifications were economical to build, since the labor was provided free, a quid-pro-quo from members of the community they were meant to protect. When fortifications became castles, they eventually involved considerable expense, sometimes costing a

BELOW: **A Norman knight of the period of the Conquest wearing a knee-length mail shirt, or hauberk. The cross-gartered legs were unprotected.**

OPPOSITE: **A fortified town under siege is defended by soldiers with javelins, shields, and bows.**

duke or lord the bulk of his income. With the use of armored cavalry forces, heavily protected strongholds worked well to fend off Vikings, Magyars and other invaders.

By the end of the ninth century, comparatively small bands of mounted knights wearing mail armor had become the most common forces, replacing Charlemagne's massive armies. Under the pressure of constant invasion, towns that had been laid out during the Roman Empire became compressed in size and were surrounded by walls. These fortified towns provided bases from which bands of knights could operate, harassing Viking, Magyar or any other marauders.

Fortifications took a number of forms in the Middle Ages. They could be the outposts that Charlemagne had built along the borders of the Frankish kingdom. They could provide the protection for churches or monasteries. They might be designed to improve the safety of a harbor or to ensure control of a strategically placed bridge. An entire town could be fortified. A castle, however, was not simply a fortification. The great age of castle-building lasted for about 600 years, from 900 A.D. to 1500 A.D.

A Legacy from the North

The Medieval castle is in many ways a legacy of the Viking invasions of Frankish territories in Western Europe starting in the ninth century. Charlemagne had succeeded in keeping the Vikings at bay by building fortifications to garrison his soldiers and capturing the outposts these Norsemen constructed. Charlemagne's offspring were not as successful. Four generations after Charlemagne, his great-great-great grandson Charles the Simple gave the Norsemen the foothold they needed to settle permanently in Frankish territory. In 911 A.D., he ceded what is now Normandy in northwest France to the Viking leader Rollo in exchange for an agreement to stop his raids. The raiders became settlers, and Rollo, the first Duke of Normandy. The Normans turned into castle builders.

A little more than 150 years after Rollo, William, then Duke of Normandy, invaded England and conquered it. Both on the continent and in England, William the Conqueror consolidated his power through the construction of castles. Norman castles, churches and abbeys are still famous today for their architectural distinction.

The story of William's rise to power is full of intrigue. Born out of wedlock — he was sometimes called William the Bastard — he nevertheless inherited the dukedom after his father died en route home from a pilgrimage to Jerusalem. His cousin Edward the Confessor was King of England, and it is believed that when William visited England, King Edward, whose mother was Norman and who had

psallite reginfo psallite;
Quo rex omnis terre ds.
psallite sapienter;
Regnabit dns ineternum

super omnes gentes. ds
sed& super sede scamsua;
Principes populi conue
nerunt cum do abraha.

quo dii fortes terre
nimium eleuati sunt;

CANTICVM PSAL   MI FILIORVM CHORE.   xLVII.

Magnus dns et
laudabilis nimis:in
ciuitate dei nri inmon
te sco eius
Dilatans exultationes uni
uerse terre.monssion
latera aquilonis.ciui
tas regis magni
Ds ingradibus eius dino
scetur.dum suscipi& ea;
Quo ecce reges terre con
gregati sunt.&conue
nerunt inunum
Ipsi uidentes tunc ad

mirati sunt.conturbati
sunt &commoti sunt.
tremor adprehendit eos;
Ibi dolores sicut parturi
entis.inspu uehementi
conterens naues charsis;
Sicut audiuimus ita &
uidimus.inciuitate dni
uirtutum.inciuitate di
nri.ds fundauit ea ineter
num
Suscepimus ds misericordi
am tua.inmedio tepli tui;
Secundu nomen tuu ds ita

&laus tua infines terre
iustitia plenae.dextera tua
Letetur monssion &exul
tent filie iude.propter
iudicia tua dne
Circum date sion &con
plectimini eam.narrate
inturribus eius.ponite
corda ura inuirtute ei
&distribuite gradus eius.
utenarretis inprogenie
altera.nos insecla
Quo hicest dsnr ineternu
&inseculu scti.&ipse reget

himself grown up in Normandy, promised William he would succeed him as King of England.

When Harold, Earl of Wessex in England, was shipwrecked on the Norman coast in 1064 and imprisoned, William released him after Harold promised to support William in his claim to the English throne. Harold was nevertheless crowned King in 1066, after Edward died without an heir. He argued that his promise to William had been extracted under duress. William invaded England later that year. William was hardly the only claimant to the English throne, but his defeat of Harold in the Battle of Hastings was decisive.

ABOVE: **A page from an Anglo-Saxon psalter includes earlier illustrations dating from the wars with the Vikings.**

55

BELOW: In the 11th-century
embroidery now known as the
Bayeux Tapestry, mounted
Norman knights attack at the
Battle of Hastings.

A chronicler of the invasion described how a prefabricated castle was brought over by the Normans:

Then the carpenters landed, who had great axes in their hands and planes and axes hung at their sides. They deliberated and looked for a good spot to place a castle. They had brought with them in the fleet three wooden castles from Normandy in pieces, ready for framing together, and they took the materials of one of these out of the ships, all shaped and bored to receive the pins that they had brought cut and ready in large barrels. Before evening, they had finished a fine fort on English ground.

The rules of feudalism dictated that a lord's vassals did not have to provide him military support outside the boundaries of his territory. William enticed his vassals to cross the English Channel by promising to reward them well. That he did after the Battle of Hastings, by staking claim to all of England and then parceling out English land to his knights as payment for their military service. While it is hard to imagine that the castle described in the chronicle of the Battle of Hastings was as imposing as some castles, it was part of a systematic strategy on William's part to maintain his control over England. Other Norman castles were, of course, far more impressive.

The Normans were known for their castle construction even before William invaded England. In fact, Edward the Confessor had hired Norman builders to construct an abbey at Westminster. Parts of it represent the earliest known Norman architecture in England. The fortified abbey of Mont-Saint-Michel in Normandy was built by command of William the Conqueror. Once he invaded England, William had churches, castles and abbeys constructed everywhere. Many of them, including White Tower of the Tower of London, still stand. Many other examples can be found in northwest France, southern Italy and Sicily.

Symbols of Power & Wealth

Unlike a strictly military fortification, a castle was a private structure. It served as the symbol of a knight's power or wealth as well as providing a place for protection. For a number of reasons, a castle was usually quite large. It became not only a king's, lord's or individual knight's residence but also the base for his forces, their equipment and their horses. In addition, it needed to have space for visitors. Neither castle owners nor knights spent a lot of time at home in the Middle Ages. When they weren't campaigning, they were still moving from one location to another. Rulers might possess many castles, shuttling back and forth among them, and some of their vassals might have more than one. In either case, minions followed their leader or provided protection for a leader's vacant castle. The person responsible for running a castle for its owner was called the castellan.

Location was the first consideration in construction of a castle. If it was going to serve as the primary depot for a region, housing fighting forces, supplies and

TOP LEFT: **Examples of armor worn in the time of William the Conqueror (left), in about 1130 A.D. (middle), and in 1200 A.D. (right).**

ABOVE: **From a manuscript dated about 1250 A.D., crossbowmen assault a fortified city.**

treasure as well as offering protection, it would be built in a central location. Other castles doubled as border outposts. In either case, a castle was not simply a retreat. It commanded the countryside for at least a 25-mile radius. Knights garrisoned in a castle could easily patrol at least that far, and the castle itself served as a lookout post for the surrounding area. Topography was crucial. The goal was to exploit an existing natural obstacle or create a new one. Mountainous sites might seem picturesquely invulnerable, but they suffered from the liabilities caused by their remoteness: low morale, lack of ready food resources. Relief forces were apt to have as difficult a time reaching a besieged castle in the mountains as the enemy did. Sites on level ground often had the advantage of being surrounded by marsh and water. Strategically valuable sites included those by river crossings, at valley entrances, near bridges, close to towns or at ports.

The design of the castle itself was predicated on placing one obstacle after another in the way of attackers. That way each obstacle required a fight and created an opportunity to diminish the opponents' forces. The fortified abbey of Mont-Saint-Michel on the coast of Normandy used nature as its first line of defense. Perched on a rocky outcrop in the English Channel, it was accessible only during low tide.

Motte-and-Bailey Design

The most basic form of castle construction in the Middle Ages is known as motte and bailey. The motte-and-bailey castle consisted of a steep mound of earth — the motte, which originally meant turf — surrounded by a ditch. Around the top of the motte ran a wooden palisade, or fence of stakes — the bailey — usually with a tower, known as a donjon, inside. Thorns were sometimes woven around

RIGHT: **Dover Castle on the cliffs above the Strait of Dover in southeastern England is of Roman or Saxon origin.**

BELOW: **This turreted alcazar, or fortified palace, begun in the 11th century, crowns a rocky hill that rises above the Eresma River at Segovia in central Spain.**

the stakes of the palisade, creating a primitive form of barbed wire. Based on the fact that prisoners were often kept on the ground-level floor of the tower, the word donjon evolved into our modern-day "dungeon." The first donjons had just two stories, one on ground level for storage and a second to house soldiers. Later towers could reach imposing heights. The earliest surviving motte-and-bailey castle was built in 990 A.D. at Mont Glonne on the Loire River in France. One of the most detailed sources of information about motte-and-bailey castles is still the embroidery that illustrates them on the Bayeaux Tapestry in France.

Unless a castle could be built on a foundation of solid rock, a moat or ditch surrounding the castle usually provided the first obstacle to attack. It might be filled with sharpened spikes or, more commonly, water. The water made it more difficult for miners, also called sappers, to undermine the outer wall enclosing the castle, although wet soil might also weaken a castle's foundation. The late 12th-century castle Gravensteen at Ghent, in what is now Belgium, is known for its unusually wide moat. When the castle wasn't under siege, a drawbridge provided access to the interior. Once a siege got underway, the drawbridge was levered up on chains and offered a second barrier in front of the outer gate. Some drawbridges swung on a pivot. Attackers who tried to cross the moat left themselves open to barrage from the outer walls. Since the outer wall was constructed as close as possible to the edge of the moat, attackers had no foothold for the next stage of their assault, even if they did manage to cross the moat. In time the outer wall had a sloping base, called a glacis or battered plinth course, making it wider and therefore more impenetrable to battering or mining.

Battlements

On top of the wall would be a walkway — called a battlement or parapet — which allowed the castle's defenders to rain arrows or any other handy projectiles down on the enemy. Sometimes wooden scaffolding, called a hoard, was extended over the battlements to allow defenders to drop heavy stones and other missiles through slots in its flooring. By the time the Duc du Berry's castle was built at Saumur in the

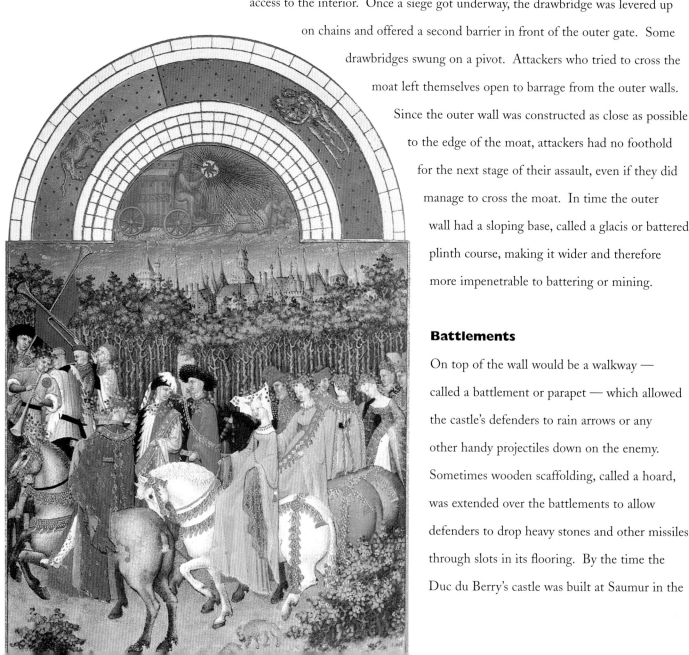

14th century, it had machicolated battlements: extensions made out of stone in place of wooden hoards.

The battlement consisted of an alternating pattern of solid walls, called merlons, and openings, known as embrasures or crenels. The familiar, crenellated design of the battlement gave a line of archers alternating spots from which to take aim and seek protection. The battlement remained a risky perch for castle defenders, so the basic design was sometimes modified to make it safer. After the 12th century, merlons had arrow-loops to allow archers to shoot directly through them. Arrow-loops varied according to the type of weapon they were designed for. A plain, vertical opening was for bow and arrow. Since crossbows were fired horizontally, they required horizontal openings, leading to cruciform-shaped arrow-loops called croslets. Embrasures acquired shutters to protect the archer while he took aim. Battlement towers positioned at the corners of the outer wall gave the castle's defenders a protected view along the wall and a position from which to take aim at the attackers' flanks.

Inside the Killing Ground

Inside the outer wall, the next obstacle would be an open space, sometimes called a killing ground, designed to confine the enemy if they breached the outer wall. That way potential invaders could once again be subjected to concentrated attack.

TOP: **Warwick Castle on the Avon in England was begun in the 14th century on the site of a 10th-century fortress.**

ABOVE: **Besieged ladies throw stones from embrasures in a castle's battlement.**

After another ditch — this one probably had sharpened stakes in it — another wall, or bailey, provided yet another obstacle. It was built higher than the outer wall, so that the castle defenders could shoot down on anyone who managed to come over or through the outer wall. The place of last resort was the donjon or, as it came to be called in later eras, keep.

The keep was a highly fortified tower, which doubled as the principal residence. It might have walls as thick as 20 feet and could reach imposing heights. Guy's Tower at Warwick Castle in England rose to 128 feet. In some parts of Europe, castles had great halls rather than towers as their chief defensive feature, but the advantage of a tower was that it could not be knocked down and it didn't take many knights to defend it. The keep was where the castle's treasure was stored. It usually had only one entrance, located above ground level. Windsor Castle in England was built with what is called a shell-keep, created by constructing a stone wall around the crown of the motte. Shell-keeps were an alternative when the ground was not suited to the weight of a complete tower.

Keeps were often eliminated in castles built after the 13th century. Not until cannons acquired enough firepower in the 16th century did a truly effective means of penetrating a castle's defenses come about. Nor did it necessarily take a large

force of knights to defend a castle successfully. Crowmarsh Castle in England was once defended by 160 men; Chaumont in France by 135, and LeMans, also in France, by 90. In 1216 only three knights, supported by 10 sergeants, were able to defend Oldham Castle in England for a week.

Construction

Castles are usually thought to be constructed from stone, but there were very few stone castles until the 12th century. They might be wooden or a combination of wood and stone, which proved stronger than either by itself. The building materials depended in part on what was available. In England and the British Isles, 11th- and 12th-century towers were commonly built of wood, while 10th-century towers in Anjou, now part of France, were made of stone. Building from stone could be time-consuming and expensive. Château Gaillard, built by Richard I, took three years to build and still wasn't finished when its owner died in 1199. Repairs were necessary and costly, especially after a siege. Many castles have separate parts dating from entirely different periods.

Stone castles had a core of rubble faced with ashlar, stone that was hewn into squares. Stone for the Tower of London was imported from Caen in Normandy, now part of France, because it was soft and easy to work with, hardening once in place. One side effect of sieges against stone castles was that the intense heat created by incendiary weapons could be enough to vitrify the stones, making them almost hard as steel. An advantage to timber when used in combination with tamped dirt was that it proved to be fireproof. Like early Greek sculpture, castles were not the drab natural colors we think of. They were usually painted in brilliant colors — red, blue and green. Conway Castle in England had a bent rectangular hall with a bright blue roof. White Tower in the Tower of London was so named because its white color was visible for miles. When it was Henry III's residence, he was concerned enough about the pristine appearance of the Tower of London that he had the rain spouts lengthened so their effluent would not stain the white-washed walls.

The shape of the castle varied by time and location. Castles were commonly square in the 12th century and round later on. The lower castle at Poitiers in France has a rare triangular shape. Château Gaillard, overlooking the Seine River in France from a 300-foot promontory, was wedge shaped, the better to deflect artillery missiles. Chepstow Castle in England, used in the 11th century for the conquest of South Wales, follows the banks of the Wye River like a snake. In time, experience with mining proved that eliminating corners made it harder to under-

ABOVE: **The storming of Warwick Castle on the Avon in central England. Today, the castle remains largely intact.**

mine a wall, and castle walls or at least their towers became round. The Tower of London has an 11th-century square donjon in the center, but its 13th-century outer walls have round towers at intervals.

Symmetry & Entrances

Symmetry grew to be a valued aesthetic for castles, and Beaumarais in Wales provides an extreme example of symmetry in design. Warkworth in England has a 15th-century keep in the shape of a Greek cross. Parapets were likely to be built from wood until the 13th century. After that, most walls had stone parapets, as was the case with Château Gaillard. As the design of castles evolved, their architects worried less about protection on all sides and instead planned serial barriers, one in front of the other, to rebuff assaults from one direction. The barbican was one such barrier and was developed to act as an enclosed killing ground in front of the castle's gatehouse.

As castle design grew increasingly sophisticated, much attention was paid to the entrance. One strategy was to place it so as to compel attackers to turn right and leave their unprotected side vulnerable. Like a maze or an obstacle course, the entrance road to a castle would funnel attackers through a series of hazards. Over time, some castles were absorbed into larger complexes of buildings that became fortified towns surrounded by walls. Most of those situated near populated areas have been torn down, however, in the name of progress.

A 19th-century reconstruction, Carcassonne in France, provides a good example of what such a Medieval fortified town looked like. Parts of the city walls date back to the sixth century, when the town was controlled by Visigoths. The inner wall and citadel were built in the 11th and 12th centuries. The main gateway, called the Narbonne Gate, had two barbicans with a narrow approach path between them. Ditches protected three sides, and the fourth had an extended battlement leading to a round barbican near the Aude River.

Perhaps the saddest part of castle sieges concerns what inevitably happened to the residents of the surrounding areas. If they took refuge in the castle, they might be temporarily safe. But when the siege went on too long and food supplies started to run out, they became a liability to the castle's defenders and were usually pushed out the front entrance by the hundreds. A kind-hearted siege leader might let these innocent bystanders pass through his lines. During the siege of Calais in 1346, Edward III allowed non-military personnel to pass, giving them food and money. More often, though, non-combatants expelled from the castle got caught in cross-fire. If they survived their race across the killing grounds, they still faced starvation, since the surrounding area had most likely been picked clean of food.

ABOVE: **A beffroy, or wheeled siege tower, with a battering ram and five platforms bearing armored knights.**

The Art of Siegecraft

When he was actively campaigning, Charlemagne revived the Roman and Macedonian practice of using siege trains to attack hostile fortifications. Dismantled siege machinery could be transported and erected on the spot, as needed. The goal of a siege was to surround an enemy fortification, cut off its supplies and communication and wait until starvation and the lack of water or ammunition led to surrender. It was essentially a passive strategy that required patience, in short supply when warriors had crops at home to worry about. A canny leader imported large quantities of wine, sporting dogs and other diversions to keep his forces occupied.

The first step in a siege was to surround the fortification so that escape was not possible. The area adjacent to the fortification would be scoured to capture all available resources and preclude their use by those inside. When the defenders of a fortification had warning of an impending siege, they were well advised to remove all supplies from the surrounding area. Then they provided for themselves and left nothing for the enemy. The siegers were apt to give up rather than face starvation.

Although the basic siege strategy of waiting was essentially foolproof, attacking knights often tried to speed up the process with forays and encounters intended to demoralize the opponents. Dirt and brush would be used, if necessary, to fill in the ditch surrounding the fortification. Or it could be drained. Otherwise, a portable drawbridge might be brought in. Scaling the walls, known as escalade, might be accomplished in a variety of ways. Some agile attackers simply climbed up, hand over hand. Others used ropes, lassoing a frenel on the battlement. Ladders provided the quickest access to the walls of the fortification, but any of these methods left the attackers vulnerable to retaliation. Towers on wheels, called beffroys or belfries, provided protection and access. Sometimes made from ships' timbers, they would be wheeled into place with knights at the ready to engage the enemy. Some were even made to float. Beffroys often had several platforms, so that the fortress would be hit by one wave of attackers after another. The Romans used beffroys that reached as high as 20 stories. The beffroys were draped with wet, untanned hides — flesh side out — to prevent defenders from setting them on fire. Vinegar and even urine — because it contains potash — were used to quench fires.

The fortification's defenders would use wooden beams to push beffroys away from the walls, or they might construct scaffolding to keep them at bay. Another ploy was to conceal pits that the beffroy might fall into. Once inside, the attackers could open the main gate and let in the rest of their forces. Storming the walls, however, left siegers open to retaliation. Defenders might pour down pitch or oil, shoot burning arrows or toss lit torches or even animal carcasses and prisoners.

Battering Rams

An alternative to scaling the walls of a castle was to destroy them. Picks could be used to hack away the outer wall of the fortification and make a breach. One of the oldest methods was to use a battering ram. A ram consisted of a wooden beam or tree trunk capped in iron, sometimes with one or more boring points. The ram was suspended by chains from a wooden frame on wheels. The iron head of the ram might actually be fashioned to look like sheep's horns, and these lumbering implements acquired nicknames like the sow or the cat. The goal was to wheel the ram into position and have sappers subject the castle wall or — even better — a gate to battering and boring. The best defense against a battering ram was to build thicker walls. Otherwise, bundles of straw or wool might be lowered into place to soften the impact of blows. Other tactics of retaliation included disabling the head of the ram by entangling it in ropes or chains or barraging the men operating it with rocks, garbage or boiling water. The tortoise or testudo — sometimes called a mouse — was a slanted roof on wheels. With metal bands armoring its roof, it was developed as a form of protection for battering rams.

Burrowing under the outer walls of a fortification was a popular and effective means of castle attack. A tortoise could be used to provide protection to diggers,

and a diversionary attack might be mounted elsewhere so it could be put in place without retaliation. As earth was removed from under the wall, temporary wooden props would be put in place to protect the miners. Once a large enough section of the fortification wall was undermined, the attackers would start a fire to burn away the props and make the wall collapse.

The best defense against mining was to build the fortification on a solid rock foundation, or surround it with a water-filled moat. One safeguard for defenders was to build the walls of a fortification so wide at the bottom that it became very difficult to undermine them. Another option was to dig a counter-mine, repel the underminers and refill the cavity. Water and smoke were effective devices for ridding an exposed mine of its sappers. The liability of counter-mining, however, lay in the danger of speeding up the process of wall collapse or the possibility of providing an entry route to attackers.

As early as 510 B.C., the Persians used brass shields to detect tunneling. The brass vibrated when placed over ground that was mined. An anti-mining strategy adopted by knights after the Crusades had taken them to the Middle East was to put pans of water on the ground. When sappers were at work underneath, the surface of the water rippled.

The lengths to which sappers might go is illustrated by the way in which the keep of Château Gaillard in France was said to have been breached. The sapper, who was a strong swimmer, filled pitchers with live coals and sealed the containers, swimming with them underwater until he reached the river side of the castle ramparts. Since the castle's defenders had no reason to think they were vulnerable there, they didn't see or prevent the sapper from igniting the wood of the ramparts, palisade and nearby houses.

Siege Artillery

Another form of siegecraft consisted of missile-throwing engines or artillery. The simplest of these were the catapult and the sling. Primitive as these weapons might seem, they were capable of causing serious damage, and it was easy enough to quarry ammunition for them. During the six-month siege of the English castle Kenilworth in 1266, the barrage of stones from slings and catapults was so heavy that missiles collided continuously in mid-air. A ballista was a machine

HE LANGLOIS. DEL   A KOHL SC

that could propel javelins, or large arrows. Functioning like a giant crossbow, it consisted of a wooden framework with a horizontal launcher of twisted rope and sinew — horsehair and human hair were the most tensile — that could be tightened or pulled back by a windlass and released, sending the javelin on its way by means of released tension. As early as 49 B.C., the Romans launched 12-foot, iron-tipped spears using ballistas. The Vikings used ballistas during the siege of Paris in 885-6 A.D.

The Mangonel

Mangonels were machines used to toss stones and other objects from vertical arms. Rocks as heavy as 500 pounds might be hurled by torsion at a wall or lobbed over it in hopes of damaging buildings inside or injuring the enemy. The mangonel's range was about 200 yards. The word for our modern weapon of choice, the gun, evolved out of mangonel. The trebuchet was the largest missile-throwing machine used in siegecraft. It employed a long, vertical lever with a counterweight at one end and a leather sling at the other. Whatever objects were placed in the sling — even beehives came in handy as missiles — were launched by the counterweight, which whipped the arm forward until it struck a cross-beam, flinging its payload at the enemy. First used in China, the trebuchet was probably introduced to Western Europe by Moorish invaders, but it was not employed there until the 12th century.

Incendiary devices played a significant role in siege artillery, and even pigeons might carry mixtures that ignited when they landed inside the castle. One of the more common uses of Greek fire, the highly flammable mix of naphtha and sulphur quicklime, was for incendiary arrows, and the substance could be blown through tubes. The formula for Greek fire variously employed oil, bitumen, naptha or resin. Sulphur made the mixture stick to a surface. Pitch made it burn longer. Quicklime made it ignite when wet, and used by itself could blind an opponent or penetrate his armor. Even heated sand could be tossed at an armored knight, penetrating his visor and burning his face or blinding him.

Starvation was the ultimate siege weapon. The defenders of a fortification might agree to negotiating terms of surrender, based on a deadline for when help might still arrive to rescue them. Knights who found themselves victims of a siege were more apt to take desperate measures first, ejecting all but essential personnel from the fortification or slaughtering their own horses for food.

Romantic as English and European castles may seem to the tourists who visit them today, when subjected to siege they set the scene for immense suffering and loss of life. The code of chivalry emerged in the Middle Ages almost as a necessity in a world that was otherwise bound by brutality.

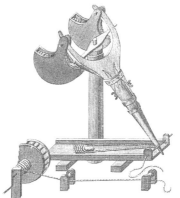

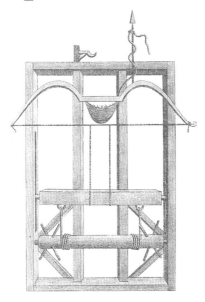

ABOVE: **Two siege mangonels, catapults employed to hurl stones from vertical arms, and a bowlike device that could launch missiles from a leather sling.**

Knightly Ideals: The Code of Chivalry

The chaos and carnage of knightly warfare during the Middle Ages could not go unchecked indefinitely. Standards of ethical behavior for the conduct of knights began to develop. When fully evolved, they were called the code of chivalry. These ideals served as an important and much-admired element of knighthood. Indeed, an extensive body of stories and legends about chivalric deeds has grown up to accompany knighthood. They have embroidered on the history of the period and inspired artists and writers from the eras that followed, long after the age of the knight came to an end.

The term chivalry is derived from *chevalier,* the French word for knight. Charlemagne's ninth century edicts governing the obligations and behavior of his knights illustrate how kings and nobles attempted from an early stage to maintain order and set the standards for knighthood. By the 12th century, ordinances of war like those issued by Frederick Barbarossa of Germany set forth strict rules of behavior. But the Church also played an important role.

By the 10th and 11th centuries in the Frankish kingdom, the Church conducted a series of conferences, which served as a Medieval counterpart to modern-day ecumenical councils. Out of these ecclesiastical assemblies came decrees known as the Pax Dei, or Peace of God. The Peace of God began as a way to protect churches from pillaging and clergymen from attack. Soon a knight who also used violence against any peasant or merchant was to be excommunicated. The Peace of God was promulgated at open-air convocations of a region's nobles, knights and peasants. The participants swore an oath to peace on a saint's relic, since most of them couldn't read or write. In the spirit of a latter-day revival meeting, acts of healing were performed to signify the holiness of the occasion.

The Church's concern over the level of violence in Frankish society went even further than the Pax Dei.

BELOW: **Frederick I, or Frederick Barbarossa, Holy Roman Emperor (1155-90).**

OPPOSITE: **Emperor Frederick Barbarossa and his two sons Henry, later Henry VI, noted for taking custody of Richard I of England in 1193, and his brother Henry of Suavia.**

70

Knights were urged to end the settling of differences in private wars and to outlaw altogether that form of altercation. Such a complete ban was probably unenforcible. In 1027, Church councils began to call for a Treuga Dei, or Truce of God. The Truce of God was, in effect, a modified ceasefire. No one was to engage in fighting during harvest, from August 15 to November 11. Nor was there to be any bloodshed on holy days or from Wednesday or Thursday night to Monday morning of each week. Again, the punishment was excommunication. Eventually, a period of 80 days a year was set aside by the Church as the time for private, or feudal, fighting. By the 12th century, the Truce of God had spread from the Frankish kingdom to Germany, Belgium and Italy, and it became part of civil as well as ecclesiastical law.

Quidabis nos pane lacrimarum: 11
potum dabis nobis in lacrimis in

Training for Knighthood

The chivalric code established standards that went far beyond considerations of when or where a knight could fight. It governed the conduct of his life from the time when, as a boy, he began to train for knighthood. It was based in ancient martial customs of initiation that had long since established an induction ceremony for entering military service. It also formalized the rite of passage from boyhood to manhood. Early Germanic tribes had marked the occasion with a gift of arms to a new young soldier from his father, a relative or his tribal chieftain. Charlemagne conferred knighthood on his son Louis at the age of 13 in 791 A.D. by girding on his son's sword for him. Such a gesture represented one of the earliest methods of conferring knighthood.

By the 12th century, a knight was not merely a soldier in service to the nobility. He had become the member of a distinct social class of warriors. Knights came from aristocratic families who held titles and owned land. Because of the expense involved in equipping a knight — horses, armor, weapons — the first son of a family was usually the only one who aspired to knighthood. Younger sons had to find other means of livelihood, like the Church or agriculture. The expensive ritual of knighting was a time when it was considered appropriate for a family's vassals to help subsidize the event by making a contribution.

The training for knighthood began as early as seven or eight years of age, when a boy might enter service as a page. At 12 or 14, he became a squire, attending a specific knight not just in battle but by waiting on him at meals or helping him dress. A significant portion of his education was based on imitation. He learned from the lord he served how to fight and conduct himself in knightly fashion. As in

TOP: **Shooting the long bow at a target. The drawing is from the Luttrell Psalter of about 1340 A.D.**

ABOVE: **Upon his arrival, a knight is bathed by his host's servants.**

all forms of military training, a knight-in-training's regimen emphasized discipline, skills development and physical fitness. The French marshal Jean de Boucicaut was known for his regular exercise and attention to breathing. In full armor, he could turn a somersault, leap onto his horse or climb a ladder using only his hands.

Treatises on Chivalry

By the late 12th century, a body of literature outlining chivalric codes began to appear. Probably the three most important such treatises were an anonymous French poem — predating 1250 — entitled *The Order of Chivalry,* Ramon Lull's 13th-century *Book of the Order of Chivalry* and the 14th-century French knight Geoffrey de Charny's *Book of Chivalry.* This tradition of treatises promoted chivalry as a code independent of religious considerations. Instead, it fed a more secular appreciation for the color and regalia of the courtly world. Treatises on chivalry were especially popular during the middle of the 14th century. Some emphasized the training necessary for knighthood. Others focused on differing interpretations of the rituals and symbols of knighthood or the hierarchy of knights. They shared an ethos fused out of aristocratic, military and Christian elements.

A knight's training culminated in a ceremony of knighting. The ceremony became over time both elaborate and symbolic. The simple one-to-one analogies

of symbolism provided an important dimension of security in Medieval life. The knighting ceremony began the day before the actual event with fasting and a bath, sometimes in specially prepared rose water. The bath symbolized that the knight was undergoing a second baptism. Thereafter he could be called a "knight of the bath," in contrast to "knights of the sword," who had won their knighthood as a reward on the battlefield. The evening was spent in church, where the knight-to-be confessed his sins to a priest, heard mass, received communion and listened to a sermon on the duties of knighthood. He then went to bed, sleeping what was called the repose of paradise.

On the day of his dubbing, the knight-to-be was dressed by attendants in a white robe meant to signify the cleanliness of his body. Next came a red cloak to indicate his readiness to shed his own blood for the Church. His outer garment was black to represent the death he must bravely face. Brown stockings symbolized the earth to which he would return at death. Around his waist went a white belt to signal his virginity.

ABOVE: **Dubbing a worthy "knight of the sword" on the field of battle.**

The Dubbing Ceremony

The dubbing ceremony itself had its origins in secular tradition and did not necessarily take place in a church. The earliest account of a dubbing ceremony in 1128 by Geoffrey the Fair of Anjou, for example, makes no mention of the Church's role. And in Germany knights never were dubbed in a church. Over time the Church began to take a more active role, though, until eventually even the Pope would confer knighthood. The Church never dominated the ceremony of knighthood, however, the way it did with the installation of kings. Dubbing was usually performed by another knight or sometimes by a lady. The sponsor presented the inductee with a sword, which symbolized the shape of the cross. The sword's two edges served to remind the knight-to-be that justice and loyalty were two sides of the knight's power.

If the ceremony was being conducted in a church, the inductee proceeded to the altar. There a priest removed the sword from where it hung around the knight-to-be's neck, placed it on the altar and blessed it. The sponsor rose and asked the inductee, "For what purpose do you wish to enter knighthood?" He took an oath to follow four commandments: never to consent to lies or treason; always to honor women and be ready to serve them; to go to mass every day; and to fast on Fridays in memory of Christ.

When his oath had satisfied his sponsor, the inducted knight received an accolade from the sponsor, who tapped his neck or shoulder three times with the flat of a sword. He might also receive a collée, a light blow of the hand or a punch. The

accolade and collée were meant to make sure the new knight never forgot the experience of dubbing. They also signified the last insults the initiate could receive without retaliating. Dubbing was usually accompanied by a phrase from the sponsor, like "Be thou a good knight," or "In the name of God, St. Michael and St. George I make you a knight." The new knight's response might be "So shall I be, with God's help."

Knightly Equipage & Its Symbolism

Those in attendance at the ceremony would arm the new knight with a mail byrnie or hauberk, breastplate, armlets, gauntlets or gloves, greaves or leg armor and helmet. Each had symbolic import: for example, the helmet demonstrated a knight's dread of shame; the byrnie or hauberk helped him resist vice and fault; the greaves kept him from straying. A horse was usually given to him as well as armor. After a sword, gold spurs were the most important gift offered to the new knight. They symbolized that he would be as swift as his spurred steed to follow God's will. Only a knight could wear gold spurs; squires wore silver spurs. At the end of the ceremony, the new knight was expected to shower his attendants and friends with gifts to mark the occasion. Feasting and celebration followed.

The dubbing ceremony was usually timed to occur on a Church holiday, such as Christmas, Easter, Pentecost or Whitsunday. A major family event, such as a marriage, provided another occasion for knighting. A special journey — to Rome, for example, to attend an emperor's coronation — might also give a vassal the necessary occasion for knighting. To be knighted on the bridge over the Tiber River in Rome had the advantage of combining knighthood with the prestige of the empire and ancient Roman tradition. Achieving knighthood during a pilgrimage to Jerusalem created yet another favorite occasion, and the eve of a major fight always produced knighting ceremonies. A warrior just knighted could be expected to fight aggressively and bravely.

Knightly honor was conferred through association by choosing to be knighted by a particularly prestigious knight. When describing his knighting to his son, Ghillebert de Lannoy emphasized that it had been done by the highly respected German knight Ruffe von Pallen during a Polish campaign. After the beginning of the 12th century, special mass ceremonies were sometimes held, when a number of aspiring

OPPOSITE: **An inducted knight receiving the accolade from his sponsor.**

ABOVE: **A portrayal of Edward the Black Prince in armor, from a play advertisement published in 1777.**

BELOW: **An 11th-century-type prick spur.**

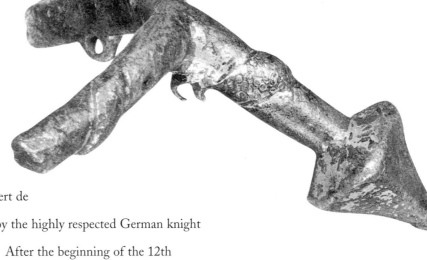

ABOVE: **A late 15th-century painted tournament shield portraying the chivalric ideal of courtly love: "You or Death."**

knights gathered to be initiated by a king or prestigious lord. Alexander III was accompanied by 20 other initiates when his father-in-law, King Henry III of England, knighted him. In Mainz on the Rhine River in Germany, Frederick Barbarossa built an entire city of tents and pavilions to accommodate his guests at the knighting of his two sons in 1184. Western Europe was a very open world during much of the Middle Ages, and chivalry spread rapidly through it, providing a common thread across most borders. Rituals for knighthood might vary some by country, but France remained the heart of the Medieval world of chivalry.

Attributes of Chivalry

The chivalric attributes of knighthood received considerable attention. Loyalty, already so deeply ingrained in the military ethic of the early Germanic tribes, provided the foundation for knightly demeanor. Courtesy was another crucial element. In the broadest sense, it suggested manners proper for use at court: the manners of a gentleman. Bravery was a personal attribute integral to knighthood. Generosity, or largesse, was another important quality. Knights went to great lengths to demonstrate their charitable nature, showering their attendants with gifts on important occasions and even bankrupting themselves rather than appear stingy. A knight must also be honorable, and perform deeds that earned him glory.

Humility was considered an important attribute, but its practice tended to be confined to other members of the knightly class. Mistreatment of those beneath your station was not thought inappropriate for a Medieval knight. As the chivalric code matured, devotion to a woman became another important requisite of knighthood, requiring the knight to be faithful in the service of love. In Arthurian legend — the cycles of stories based on chivalry in England — when Perceval left home to join the court of King Arthur, his mother advised him: "If you encounter near or far, a lady in distress, or any damsel in need of help, be ready to aid her if she asks you, since all honor lies in such deeds. When a man fails to honor ladies, his own honor dies."

Genealogy grew increasingly important to knighthood. A knight acquired far more prestige if he could demonstrate that he came from a line of knights. In some countries knightly lineage became one of the requirements for knighthood, and it was unacceptable to trace one's family's knighthood through the maternal side. The subtleties of the class system which underpins chivalry is illustrated by the distinction made in Germany between lineal nobility and service nobility. They continued long after the knights who had earned their status through service had established their families' noble lineage.

Conduct Toward Other Knights

Conduct towards other knights played an important role in the code of chivalry. Lacking the fully developed legal system that the modern world is accustomed to, knights resorted to trial by combat to settle personal disputes. This custom resulted in the practice of dueling, which has become a cliché of chivalrous behavior. A toss or slap of the gauntlet, or glove, challenged a knight's opponent to resolve a dispute formally.

The challenger was required to stipulate the basis for his complaint, and to ignore or reject such a challenge was a direct affront to a knight's honor. Only equals in rank could participate in a trial by combat. Women, the clergy and the disabled were exempt from these rules of combat, but they could select a champion to fight in their place. Professional champions existed as early as the 10th century. King Otto I of Germany submitted a dispute over his daughter's chastity to a duel by champions, and champions were used by embassies in the event of diplomatic quarrels.

As knights became increasingly well armored, killing them grew more difficult. The only vulnerable spot was a man's throat, and the only time it might be exposed was when he had been unhorsed and was lying on the ground, a highly unchivalrous position. Taking prisoners became a popular alternative to killing in a private dispute, and it had the advantage of providing a ransom. Once a knight was taken

ABOVE: **An attribute of chivalry, the commitment to rescue a lady in distress.**

BELOW LEFT: **Knights engaged in hand-to-hand combat. In personal disputes the code of chivalry required knights to be of equal rank.**

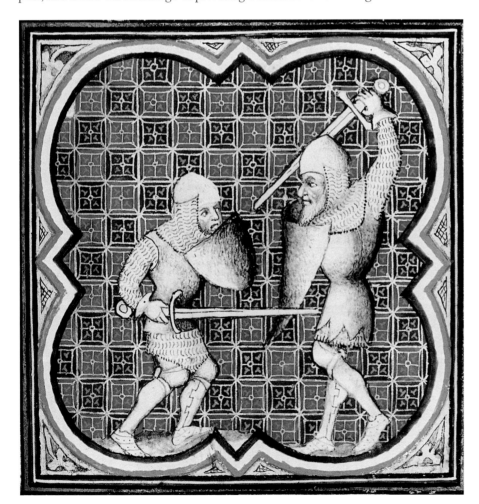

BELOW LEFT: In a page from a late 13th-century French psalter, the Old Testament David is depicted as an ideal Christian soldier.

BELOW RIGHT: A mid 14th-century English psalter portraying David and Goliath shows the association of chivalrous knights with religious figures.

prisoner, he would be released if he promised to return with a ransom by an agreed-on deadline. Some knights earned a substantial income from ransoms.

One important dimension of chivalry consisted in its mythologizing of warfare. Medieval warriors long had the habit of giving their horses and their weapons special names. The chivalric code's high standards of behavior helped turn such personifications into the stuff of legend. Charlemagne's sword was called Joyeuse, French for "joyful", and Arthur's was Excalibur. Both Charlemagne's faithful knight Roland and his sword Durendaal were immortalized in the *Song of Roland,* which tells the story of the Battle of Roncevalles in 778 A.D.

The most famous knights and their feats achieved a stature close to worship, leading to the creation of pantheons of heroes and events. Churches competed to acquire the relics of famous knights who died in battle. They also immortalized these heroes in sculptures and stained glass. The story of Roland's heroism at Roncevalles is preserved in stone at the Cathedral of Verona in Italy. The stained glass of Chartres Cathedral in France narrates the miracle of the lances that unfurled with leaves on the night before they were used by Charlemagne's knights in Spain. The heroics of famous Medieval knights became associated with legends

from antiquity and were retold to provide analogies and show how the classical tales prefigured feats of Medieval chivalry.

Old Testament Knights

Chivalrous knights also became associated with religious figures. Old Testament heroes provided exemplars of the Christian soldier. The perfect Biblical knight was said to be Judas Maccabeus. David, Abraham and Gideon were also held up as examples. To 12th- or 13th-century knights, Joshua's conquering of the Holy Land foreshadowed their own crusade to Jerusalem. In many ways, the code of chivalry helped blend two separate traditions of knighthood. One was based on the pagan practice of knights ruling the world and keeping the peace; the second saw knighthood as a God-given assignment to defend Christianity and guard its holy places. Medieval scholars traced the origin of chivalry back to the expulsion of Adam and Eve from Eden, which was identified as the time when war began. The claim was made that chivalry came about to restrain and defend the world after the Fall. Along with Charlemagne and Arthur, Godfrey de Bouillon, who helped capture Jerusalem during the First Crusade, ranked as one of the fore-most Medieval knights. Joan of Arc, the Maid of Orleans, was the only woman who achieved stature as one of the great knightly heroes.

Stories from the court of King Arthur — based on an English hero from the sixth or seventh century but written much later — were popular all over Western Europe as well as England. More so than in stories about Charlemagne's feats, the Arthurian legends took on fantastical dimensions and emphasized knight errantry, wanderings in pursuit of heroic feats in the name of love. As a part of the chivalric code, knightly love took an idealized form. While a knight might perform martial feats in the name of a lady, he did not expect a consummation of the relationship.

By the 16th century, changes in the social and political fabric of Medieval society led to the disappearance of the chivalric tradition. Soldiers had become mercenaries, and military technology had changed with the advent of firearms. Infantry replaced cavalry as the predominant troop organization. The sometimes fanciful chivalric fables about Arthur and Charlemagne faded in popularity, and the religious ardor that fueled the Crusades and with it chivalry, was replaced by Protestantism and the humanism of the Renaissance.

ABOVE: **The legendary French hero Roland, immortalized in the late 11th-century** *Song of Roland.*

LEFT: **The Sword of Tenure of Battle Abbey, c. 1420. William the Conqueror built the abbey to commemorate his victory at Hastings.**

The Crusades: The Knightly Mission

Toward the end of the 11th century, the primary arena for world conflict shifted away from Western Europe and the struggles of its knights to the Middle East. Jerusalem had been captured 400 years earlier by Omar, advisor to the great Islamic leader Mohammed. At first the Christian world had little cause for worry because pilgrims continued to have access to their holiest of cities. Then early in the 11th century, control of Jerusalem shifted to a Fatimite sect, so-named because its members claimed to be descendents of Mohammed's daughter Fatima. The Turkish Fatimite Moslems began persecuting Christian pilgrims. In 1010 they destroyed the Church of the Holy Sepulchre in Jerusalem. Concern mounted in the Christian world.

Since the fourth century A.D., pilgrimages to the Holy Land offered Christians an important way of doing penance. As one of the sacraments of the Roman Catholic Church, penance was the means an individual had to be absolved of sin. The violence and bloodshed of the knight's profession made him a ready candidate for relieving his soul of guilt by doing penances. Gradually, the prospect of Jerusalem being in the hands of infidels became intolerable to Western European knighthood.

There was also concern over the inroads of Islam closer to home. From before the time of Charles Martel in the eighth century, Moorish domination of the Iberian peninsula — now Spain and Portugal — had motivated Frankish knights to free the region from Islam's grip. By 1030, the Iberian Moslem leadership was fragmented, creating an open invitation for invasion. Eleventh-century reconquest of the Iberian peninsula started as a series of individual campaigns by Western European knights to conquer new territory. The Church saw to it that newly conquered land in the Iberian Peninsula was held in fiefdom to the See of St. Peter. Eventually the Iberian campaigns became part of a wider movement against the Islamic threat.

Other parts of Western Europe under

ABOVE: **An early 13th-century stone figure from Rheims Cathedral, probably a contemporary Byzantine warrior wearing scale armor.**

Islamic influence were targeted. Norman knights established themselves in Italy, retaking Sicily from Moslem control, and knights from the Italian city-states of Genoa and Pisa ejected Moslems from Sardinia. The general struggle against Islam reached its first real crisis in 1071. At that point, Seljuk Turkish Moslems took control of Jerusalem after defeating the army of the Byzantine Empire — representing the eastern branch of the Catholic Church — at Manzikert in what is now Turkey. The Holy City was no longer safe for pilgrims, and knights in the Christian world began girding themselves to make a massive response to the expansion of Islam.

The reformist pope Gregory VII laid the groundwork for the Roman Catholic Church's intervention in what had previously been the exclusive domain of knighthood: warfare. Rejecting centuries of essentially pacifist Church policy, Gregory argued that a knight's loyalty to the Church came first, before loyalty to his lord. He called knights "vassals to St. Peter." When the Byzantine Emperor Michael VII appealed to him for help in rebuffing Turkish and other Moslems, Gregory wrote to King Henry IV, then Holy Roman Emperor, and proposed that Henry mount an expedition to rescue the Byzantine Empire. That was not to happen until years later, but the connection between a knight's duties to the Church and his role as a soldier was cemented. The shift to a warlike Church had profound consequences for knighthood. It involved a strategy to divert the energies of knighthood away from royal and baronial disputes.

The Council of Clermont

In 1095 Byzantine Emperor Alexius sent representatives to Pope Urban II, appealing to him to send knights who could help recapture territory taken from the Byzantine Empire by Turkish moslems and other "infidels." The Pope was eager to repair the split between the Roman and Eastern Catholic churches. He laid the groundwork carefully, visiting Western European knighthood's leadership in what is now northern Italy and southern France to win its support. Late in November of that year, he preached before thousands gathered in Clermont, in what is now southeast France, as part of a Church council. His words changed history and gave knighthood a sacred mission:

> *Enter upon the road to the Holy Sepulchre; wrest that land from a wicked race, and subject it to yourselves. Jerusalem is a land fruitful above all others, a paradise of delights. That royal city . . . implores you to come to her aid. Undergo this journey with enthusiasm for the remission of your sins, and be assured of your reward in the imperishable glory of the Kingdom of Heaven.*

In a frenzy of tears and feet-stamping, the crowd shouted in response, "God wills it!" Urban urged them to turn the phrase into their battle cry. He passed out crosses and called on all who joined the crusade to sew crosses on their clothing in recognition of the holiness of the mission.

Ademar, a bishop who had first been trained as a knight, came forward and vowed to take up the cause. The Pope appointed him leader of the First Crusade. Count Raymond IV of Toulouse was the first knight to vow to go to Jerusalem. Nobles, knights and thousands of peasants followed Ademar and Raymond and took up the holy cause. Urban traveled from city to city — Tours, Bordeaux, Toulouse, Montpellier, Nimes — for the next eight months, spreading the word about the pilgrimage to Jerusalem.

An Army of Thousands

Thousands more recruits pledged to crusade and joined the sacred army. In part it was a response to papal promises of pardons for sins to all killed in the attempt to free the Holy Land. The Church assumed legal and social responsibility for the

crusading army. Peasants were released from their feudal obligations, taxes were forgiven, interest on loans was waived, prisoners were freed and death sentences were commuted to a lifetime of service in the Holy Land. Religious fervor was just one of many sources for the overwhelming response to take up the cause of Christianity. For the thousands of knights who went — modern historians set the number at about 4,000 — there was also the lure of adventure, the chance to be a hero and the prospects for booty. The Church gave knights who took the vow to crusade mortgages or bought their land outright to finance their excursion to the Holy Land. Putting up his Norman duchy as collateral, one knight, Robert Curthose, borrowed the money from his brother King William of England.

For second- or third-born sons of knights with no opportunity to inherit family property, the crusade held out the promise of acquiring their own estates. Baldwin of Bologne, one of the leaders of the First Crusade, was landless before he went to the Holy Land. Even though the prestige of knighthood had increased rapidly over the centuries, its economic status had not. The inheritance system diluted a family's wealth. In noble families, inheritances were traditionally divided equally among the offspring of a knight. Eventually the point was reached where such divisions meant no single family member inherited enough land to survive on, let alone to equip himself as a knight. Of necessity, the system changed to one of undivided inheritance.

One form was fraternal, in which all male offspring inherited their father's property collectively. The estate was administered by just one, who served as the new head of the family, and the other siblings became his dependents. The most common new form of inheritance was primogeniture, which meant the eldest son inherited his father's entire estate. Either way, only one son could expect to acquire through inheritance the means that would assure his knighthood. The others might join a religious order or stay at home, but not if they wanted true independence. A military campaign in the Holy Land offered that independence.

The People's Crusade

A giant wave of grass-roots activism was washing over Western Europe. The contributing factors were several. The weight of the feudal system had begun to grow heavy on those at the bottom of the economic ladder, and a rising population created further pressures. Western Europe had experienced a series of crop failures. The Pope set August, 1096, as the date of departure for the First Crusade. So great was the fervor of many would-be Crusaders that they did not wait. Two charismatic leaders, a cleric named Peter the Hermit and a German knight named Walter the Penniless, started the journey from France to the Holy Land with 12,000 Crusaders in the spring of 1096. Another group, estimated at about 5,000, left from Germany under the leadership of a priest named Gottschalk. Count Emico of Germany led a third company. More enthusiastic than prepared, these early Crusaders had little training and carried as weapons only the tools of their trades: hay forks, axes and scythes.

On their way through Germany and Bohemia, now Czechoslovakia, some of these early, overzealous Crusaders persecuted Jews and were dispersed by the King of Hungary. Lacking proper provisions, the hungry Crusaders pillaged from peasants and villagers who should have been their allies. Walter the Penniless's army sacked Belgrade, then part of Bulgaria and now of Serbia, and was attacked by Bulgarian troops. The early Crusaders arrived at Constantinople, capital of the

Byzantine Empire and now Istanbul in Turkey, with their numbers greatly depleted by fighting, famine, fever and plague. The Byzantine Emperor Alexius, expecting a disciplined force of knights rather than a rag-tag, unruly band of peasant men, women and children numbering in the thousands, did not provide them adequately with food. So they broke into churches and palaces to help themselves. Alexius sped them on their way by providing ships to cross the Bosporus straits into Asia Minor.

Alexius also advised the leaders of this "people's crusade" to wait until the main body of Crusaders arrived before mounting a military operation. Instead these early Crusaders decided to attack the city of Nicaea. Part of the old Roman Empire, the prosperous city of Nicaea had been captured by Turkish Moslems in 1078. The people's Crusaders, including leader Walter the Penniless, were slaughtered by Turks armed with bows and arrows. Another leader, Peter the Hermit, returned to Constantinople before the attack and later returned in disgrace. The campaigns of the people's Crusaders sadly made little or no military impact.

Bona fide knights who had taken the cross prepared more carefully and arrived later. None of Western Europe's kings participated. Philip I of France, William II of England and Henry IV of Germany had all been excommunicated for various offenses connected to the Church. The majority of knights who fought in the First Crusades were Frankish noblemen. Duke Godfrey of Bouillon, now

BELOW: **Map showing the routes of the First, Second, and Third Crusades.**

part of Belgium, was both a military man and a monk, religious to the point of fanaticism. The Norman count Bohemond of Taranto, now in Italy, traveled with his nephew Tancred, immortalized in the Italian poet Tasso's epic, *Jerusalem Delivered*. Frankish count Raymond of Toulouse had already fought against the Moslems in Spain and led the largest contingent of knights. Wives and families, reluctant to leave their husbands behind and miss the historic occasion, joined the Crusade. Stirred by Pope Urban's preaching, Italian merchants and sailors provided the necessary supplies.

Most knights came with their own armor, weapons and horses. Exceptions were Bohemond and his nephew Tancred, who subsidized all the knights who traveled with them. Raymond of Toulouse set up a fund for equipment replacements, and some knights bought Arabian horses en route to Jerusalem.

Five Armies of True Knights

Each of the Frankish nobles organized a separate force of trained knights that made its way to the staging point, Constantinople. A total of five armies of knights was massed. The result of such autonomy created the most serious military weakness of the Crusades: they had no single commander-in-chief. The first knight to arrive in Constantinople was King Philip I of France's brother, Hugh of Vermandois, from what is now northern France. The boat that was carrying him was shipwrecked off the Adriatic coast, but he made his way from there to Constantinople and was greeted by Emperor Alexius. Many were suspicious of the Byzantine Emperor,

whom they thought had mistreated the earlier-arriving people's Crusaders. Storming Constan-tinople itself was considered but rejected after Emperor Alexius offered bribes, provisions, transport and military aid. In exchange, Alexius extracted oaths from all the knights except Tancred and Raymond that whatever lands they captured would be held in fealty to him as part of the Byzantine Empire.

By the beginning of 1097, some 30,000 knights gathered in Constantinople and crossed the Bosporus straits. Nicaea surrendered in June under an agreement that the city would not be sacked. The Crusaders' victory there was, in effect, sub-verted by secret negotiations between the defending garrison and representatives from Alexius. The morning of their final assault, the Crusaders saw the flag of the Byzantine Empire flying over the city and were kept from plundering.

Another pitched battle — there were few during the Crusades — was fought at Dorylaeum, now in northwest Turkey. Bohemond ordered his knights to dismount and defend the rest against the hailstorm of arrows loosed by the Turkish Moslem forces, while the Crusaders' infantry protected non-combatants. The women non-combatants carried water to the front line. When reinforcements from Count Raymond and Bishop Adhemar arrived, the Turks fled. The bodies of their horses, who had been ridden to death, were found three days further along the route.

ABOVE: **Crusaders under Godfrey of Bouillon and Tancred defeat Moslem forces of the Sultan of Egypt at Ascalon in 1099. The drawing is from a glass painting at the Abbey of Saint-Denis.**

The Siege of Antioch

Antioch, also in Turkey and one of the great cities of antiquity, was the Crusaders' next destination. They traveled in two divisions to accommodate the large number of non-combatants, which included priests, wives, children and other camp follow-ers. Their progress was unimpeded by the enemy. Many men, women, horses and dogs nevertheless died on the 500-mile trek from the heat and a lack of food and water. Overwhelmed by the heat, many knights even tried to sell their heavy armor and shields.

Ignorance of the region's geography caused serious problems. Suspicious of the Byzantines, who knew the terrain, the Crusaders often ignored their advice on what routes to follow and traveled circuitously. Raymond of Toulouse attempted to cross the Armenian mountains to Baghdad, with the result that his men and horses suffered from thirst and starvation. After crossing the Taurus Mountains in what is now Turkey, several groups of the nobles and their knights split off from the main force to make private conquests. Baldwin, Godfrey of Bouillon's brother, set up the first Latin principality in the East at the Macedonian city Edessa, now in Greece and one of the major religious centers of the Byzantine Empire before it was captured by Moslems in 639 A.D.

ABOVE: **A siege tower with a battering ram and drawbridge used by Crusaders against a Moslem fortress.**

BELOW RIGHT: **After a siege of 40 days, Godfrey of Bouillon leads his Crusaders against the 1000-man Moslem garrison at Jerusalem.**

The strategy of the knights was to organize themselves into "battles," which consisted of infantry alternating with mounted knights attacking in waves. The heavily armored, mounted knights could stand and readily defeat their Moslem opponents, but they were not able to outrun them. Western European horses were unaccustomed to the terrain and the climate, and disciplined cavalry charges did not occur until the 17th century. Combining cavalry with infantry became the key to the Crusaders defeating the Islamic forces.

Antioch Falls

When the Crusaders reached Antioch, the city was put under siege for eight months. Cold and hunger took their toll on the Crusaders. They ate horses, donkeys, camels, dogs and even rats. At least one report claims they resorted to cannibalism, slicing off the buttocks of dead Moslems and roasting them. Disease and starvation were perennial problems whenever a Medieval army camped in one location for an extended period. Sanitary conditions were poor, and supply logistics were primitive. A fleet of ships from Genoa rescued the sieging Crusaders by bringing fresh supplies. Emperor Alexius was en route with an army of Greeks, but when deserting Crusaders told him their forces had already been defeated, he turned back into Asia Minor. When the Crusaders, already mistrustful of Alexius, learned about it, they felt betrayed by him.

Then a Frankish priest claimed to have discovered a holy relic under the floor of St. Peter's Cathedral. It was supposed to be the spear that had pierced Christ's side, and it was carried aloft as a holy relic to inspire the Crusaders. An apparition of three knights dressed in white appeared, and Adhemar, the Pope's designate and leader of the crusade, declared them to be the martyrs St. Theodore, St. Maurice

and St. George. These somewhat questionable events, most likely ruses to spur the flagging Crusaders, reflect a mystical current that ran through the Crusades and worked to inspire fanatical commitment.

Just days before a force of Moslem reinforcements arrived with help, Antioch fell, and most of the Crusaders departed safely by ship for their next objective. A rumor spread that Christ had commanded the Moslem officer, who provided access to the city, to return the city to Christians. Bribery was more likely. Count Bohemond negotiated with the officer in charge of the garrison defending the Tower of the Two Sisters, who agreed to let the Crusaders in. Slaughter of the city's Moslem population and widespread looting followed.

Bohemond was named Prince of Antioch. With less-than-chivalric logic, he claimed it for himself on the grounds that Alexius's failure to arrive at Nicaea had nullified the oath he had taken in Constantinople to hold Antioch as a fief for the Byzantine Empire. Bishop Adhemar, who had served as a voice of reason in the Crusaders' dealings with the Byzantine Empire, died, most likely of typhus, and the remaining leaders of the Crusaders were hard put not to quarrel among themselves.

On to Jerusalem

After a six-month interlude of reorganization, the Crusaders headed for Jerusalem. They arrived on June 7, 1099, their number 12,000 strong. Estimates of numbers

vary widely. The Fatimid caliph of Jerusalem tried to negotiate a peace treaty by offering to guarantee the safety of Christians in his city. The offer came too late, and the Crusaders began their siege. Food was not scarce for the Crusaders, but the surrounding wells and springs had been either poisoned or filled in by the enemy so that little water was available. Siege towers, battering rams, catapults and ballistas were put in position, and the enemy threw stones, arrows, flaming straw and wood wrapped with burning pitch, wax and sulphur. The Moslem garrison of 1,000 soldiers defended the city for 40 days before capitulating to the Crusaders.

Slaughter of the 60,000 Moslems still in the city followed until the streets ran with blood. Jews were herded into a synagogue and burned alive. The priest Raymond of Agiles reported on the un-Christian scene:

Numbers of the Moslems were beheaded...others were shot with arrows or forced to jump from the towers; others were tortured for several days and then immolated in flames. In the streets were piles of heads and hands and feet.

Another chronicler described the looting and celebration:

The Crusaders ran about the city, seizing gold, silver, horses, mules and pillaging the houses filled with riches. Then, happy and weeping with joy, our men went to worship at the sepulchre of our Lord and rendered up the offering they owed.

The heads of the murdered were mounted on posts, and bodies were dismembered to search for swallowed gold pieces.

Amidst much squabbling and jockeying for position among the knights, Godfrey of Bouillon was chosen to rule Jerusalem as Defender of the Holy Sepulchre. The Latin kingdom of Jerusalem was officially formed. Moslem retaliation lay not far behind. An army of Egyptian Moslems arrived at Ascalon on the Mediterranean coast in Palestine in preparation for an assault on the Holy City. Godfrey won a victory by taking the enemy by surprise. A year later he was dead from typhoid fever, and his brother Baldwin declared himself king of Jerusalem. The new Christian kingdom was divided into four principalities, each of which became a separate fief ruled by a baron. Antioch had already been claimed by Bohemond and Edessa by Baldwin. Tripoli, now in Lebanon, was taken over by Raymond.

Creating New Christian Kingdoms

The port cities of Jaffa, Tyre, Acre, Beirut and Ascalon — now in Israel, Palestine and Lebanon — were turned over to the Italian city-states of Venice, Pisa and Genoa in exchange for naval support and supplies. The leaders of these city-states were eager to develop trade routes to the East and offered protection and support to the Crusaders. Whether Christian or Moslem, residents of the region lost all property rights and became serfs enfioffed to their new feudal lords.

After the First Crusade, most of the knights returned home. Their victories had been almost miraculous, and the First Crusade was the only truly successful one of the many that followed. The knights were fighting on terrain that was inappropriate for traditional knightly battle formations of the time, which relied on heavily armed cavalry and shock tactics. The Moslem forces had skilled archers on horseback, and they often used circular attacks to harass the wings or camp guard of their European opponents. Some knights joined the new knightly orders that were forming and stayed on. Moslem forces bided their time and nursed their desires for retaliation. Then as now, Jerusalem was as holy a city to the Moslem religion as it was to the Christian forces that had assumed control of it.

ABOVE: **A short-sleeved, knee-length mail tunic, or hauberk, with a mail hood, or coif. The tunic opens at the front, and the front and sides are reinforced with overlapping plates.**

Crusader Armor

By the time of the First Crusade, hauberks, the knee-length mail tunics that had been worn by William the Conqueror's knights when they invaded England in 1066, were standard equipment. By the 12th century, hauberks had long sleeves, and mail mittens called mufflers were added early in the 13th century.

Those that were short-sleeved were known as haubergeons. Most hauberks had tight-fitting coifs, or mail hoods, although coifs might also be made of leather or cloth. Many hauberks had a ventail, or mail flap, that covered the mouth and lower face.

Aketons, also called gambesons or pourpoints, were white cloth shirts or tunics believed to be worn under the hauberk for both protection and comfort. Sometimes aketons were even lined with rabbit fur. The vertical quilting of the aketon served as a shock-absorber. Such protection was necessary since blows that might not necessarily penetrate mail could nevertheless inflict serious injury in the form of blunt trauma with broken bones and hemorrhaging. Quilted caps were worn under coifs for the same purpose. The aketon sometimes replaced the hauberk as a linen coat, quilted with cotton, wool or rags. While it might seem to provide less protection than mail or metal plates, the aketon was an economical choice for warriors who could not afford a hauberk.

A popular alternative to mail armor was the scale hauberk. Another form of body protection was made out of leather and called the cuirie or cuirasse. Sometimes reinforced with iron, the cuirie was worn over the hauberk but under the cloth tunic that a knight wore on top of his armor. By the 13th century, cloth tunics began to be reinforced with a lining of metal plates, which can be seen from the outside by the rivets that hold them in place. Occasionally, knights wore a loose white surcoat over their hauberks. It was usually sleeveless, reached to mid-calf and had a belt or cord independent of the belt for a sword. It is thought to have been introduced to keep a crusading knight's armor from heating up in the sun or protect it from wetness. It also could display the wearer's coat of arms.

In addition to the mail sleeves that were part of the hauberk, Crusader armor also sometimes included additional protection for the arms: espaulers for the shoul-

TOP: **A conical helmet from the 10th or 11th century, of Polish or Russian origin, is made of iron plates overlaid with gilt copper and silver-capped nails.**

ABOVE: **An almost fully developed great helm of early 13th-century design worn by a knight carved in stone on the west front of Wells Cathedral in southwestern England.**

96

der and couters for the elbow. Not much is known about espaulers, but flat plates of various shapes, known as ailettes, were thought to serve as a place to display a knight's coat of arms so it was visible from the side. Because a fighter's elbow was a particularly vulnerable part of the body, the small round plates known as couters were strapped on the arm over the hauberk.

Mail protection for a knight's legs was called chausses. Long mail stockings known as hosen were braced up to a belt beneath the hauberk and gartered at the knee so that the weight of the mail would not make them drag. Sometimes mail was used to cover only the front of the leg and top of the foot. It was laced on and attached to a belt at the waist under the hauberk. Cloth stockings went underneath as liners. Gamboised cuisses protected the thighs with thick padding, sometimes extending to the middle of the calf. They were often covered with silk, velvet or embroidery. Separate knee defenses — poleyns — were saucer- or cup-shaped and made of iron. The schynbald was a metal guard for the shin. The feet were also covered with mail.

Helms & Shields

Early Crusader helms, or helmets, were usually conical in shape with a strip of metal to protect the nose called a nasal. The nasal obscured the face and sometimes made it hard to identify an individual knight. Eventually, iron guards covered the entire face. They were pierced with openings for the eyes called sights and ventilation holes called breaths. A neck-guard might make up part of the helm. The more affluent knights had helms that were studded with jewels along the brow band. By the 12th century, round-topped helms were common, either with or without nasals, and they were followed by cylindrical helms with flat or domed tops called a basinet or cervelier.

A new type of head-gear, called a kettle hat or chapel de fer, appeared in the 13th century. It was broad brimmed and roughly shaped like an inverted kettle. The brim helped protect a knight from downward cuts and deflect missiles during a siege. In any case,

it was not unusual for crusading knights not to wear any helm and rely instead on a coif for head protection.

When crusading knights did wear a helm, some method of identification became necessary. A fan-shaped attachment to the top of the helm — a crest — was used for identifying insignia, or insignia might be painted on the side of a helm. Crests might even consist of elaborate, three-dimensional models of birds or animals flanked by flags. Out of this need to identify a knight hidden in his armor developed the Medieval institution of heraldry, armorial designs used for identification. A high-ranking knight might wear a crown in place of a crest.

Shields varied from the old-fashioned round type to the kite shape that was rounded on top and elongated to protect the left side and leg of a mounted knight. A small version of the round shield, called a buckler, was commonly used by infantry but also sometimes by knights. By the time of the First Crusade, shields still had bosses, but they were no longer designed to cover the hand grip, which had been shifted off center and was used with brases or straps that went around the forearm. The guige was an adjustable leather strap that allowed the user to hang up the shield or sling it around his neck. Crusade shield surfaces were painted with a variety of icons, including crosses and winged dragons. By the second half of the 12th century, shield insignia began to be passed down from one generation to the next. A straight-topped shield was introduced in the 12th century, probably making it easier for a knight to see over the top of the shield.

Over Crusader horses went a loose cloth covering called a housing. One part covered the head of the horse and its withers or shoulders; the other covered the crupper or hindquarters behind the saddle. When this type of equine protection was made of mail, it was called a trapper. The expense and weight of such equipment limited its practicality. A saddle cloth with slots for the top of the saddle was sometimes used in the 12th century. Testiers or shaffrons were the names given to the leather or iron armor for the horse's head. Most were cloth, but horse armor of iron was referred to by the 12th century. There is evidence that Crusader horses wore a curb bit; barbarian horses had used only a snaffle.

Crusader Weaponry

Crusader knights still depended heavily on the spear or lance, but it was now held couched: tucked under the right arm and held in position by the right hand. This new position gave the weapon greater rigidity, since the strength of the knight's arm was combined with the power of the horse. The lance, 10 to 12 feet in length, was not actually couched until just before use. Until then, it was carried upright with the butt resting on the saddle. Between charges, a knight would rest the lance diagonally across the horse's neck.

Tilting with couched lances necessitated changes in the knight's saddle. A breast band, attached on each side of the saddle across the horse's chest, kept the saddle from being pushed backward by the force of the impact. Both the pommel in front and the cantle in back were built up on the saddle with arsons — extensions — to keep the rider secure in his seat. Double girths helped to protect against one of them breaking on impact, with the second one strapped over the top of the saddle. The knight rode straight-legged, nearly in a standing position, held aloft by the stirrups and kept secure by the arsons.

Swords & Daggers

The most important weapon for the crusading knight was his sword. By the Crusades it had become the symbol of chivalry. Once he charged with his lance and it was broken, a knight drew his sword and fought with it. The Norman knights often used broad-bladed swords, about three feet in length, that were similar to those carried by their Viking predecessors. Many were inlaid with the name Ingelrii, assumed to be the maker. Religious inscriptions also might be inlaid in iron with such Latin phrases as "Homo Die" or "In Nomine Domini." Sometimes letters were simply used as a repetitive pattern on a sword blade. A single-edged sword, designed like a machete, was called the falchion.

At the time of the First Crusade, a new narrower-bladed sword appeared that was slightly longer. Many of these swords were inscribed with the Latin phrase, "Gicelin me fecit" or "Gicelin made me." A third type of sword blade was broad with an even taper and sharp point. The taper made the weapon less point-heavy and easier to wield. Pommels were usually made of iron, but some were fashioned out of crystal or semi-precious stone. A baselard was a short sword or dagger. Another name for the kind of stabbing weapon apt to be used in addition

ABOVE: **The Conyers falchion, probably English, from about 1257-72. The single-edged, cleaver-shaped blade was popular with all classes of soldiers from the 13th century onward.**

ABOVE: **A selection of seven crossbow bolts, or arrows, probably German, from the early 16th century.**

BELOW: **A quiver and a pair of crossbow bolts, probably 16th-century German.**

to the sword was quillon dagger. Daggers called coustels or cultelli began to be used by foot soldiers beginning in the 12th century.

Once the Crusades got underway, the magical aura of the knight's sword was transformed into religious significance. The analogy of the sword's shape to the cross became even more important during this period, and swords continued to be used for oaths. Religious relics might be concealed in the sword's pommel to provide the owner with a saint's protection. This practice occurred as early as the time of Charlemagne, whose sword "Joyeuse" had a relic in its pommel. A tooth of St. Peter, a hair of St. Denis and a fragment of the Virgin Mary's robe were also said to be hidden the the hilt of Durendal, Roland's sword. On ceremonial occasions, a knight carried his sword sheathed, with the point facing up, as a symbol of justice.

Scabbards were decorated with images meant to be viewed in this position. When seated, a king would sit with his sheathed sword lying across his lap. After he died, a knight's sword would often be hung over his tomb.

Clubs made up another part of the crusading knight's arsenal. Some had quatrefoil heads, and others, known as gibets, were a form of the mace, or metal-headed club, that many knights used. Battle axes and gisarmes — axes with crescent-shaped blades — were popular Crusader weapons, especially for knights. The fauchard was similar to a scythe and perhaps adapted from this agricultural tool.

The Crossbow & Other Missile Weapons

The crossbow was an important weapon during the Crusades. Since William the Conqueror's invasion of England in 1066, regular bows and arrows had been more frequently used by knights. The Moslem forces were adept at their use. Also called the arblast, the crossbow required less skill than a conventional bow. It had been in existence since late Roman times. A short, heavy bowstock was made of laminated layers of wood, horn and sinew and covered with leather or parchment. It was mounted at right angles to a straight stock, called the tiller. The bowstring was cocked into a barrel-shaped catch, called the nut, on the tiller. A long lever, called the trigger, kept the bowstring in place until the archer was ready to fire his arrow or bolt. He aimed by positioning the tiller against his cheek and then pressed the trigger. The head of the bolt or arrow fired by a crossbow was usually square and called a quarrel.

By the 13th century, crossbows had become so powerful that they had to be cocked from a hook on the archer's belt. A stirrup added to the tiller enabled the archer to use his leg to cock the crossbow. The Church disapproved of the lethal crossbow, but it was one of the era's most important weapons, perhaps because it was able to withstand harsh desert conditions. Pope Innocent II even denounced the use of the crossbow in an 1139 Lateran Council proclamation, except of course against "infidels."

At the end of the 13th century a powerful new form of bow, developed in Wales, was introduced. The longbow increased the power of the ordinary bow tenfold, although its proper use required years of training and regular practice. By the 14th century the longbow replaced the crossbow and made England the strongest military presence in Western Europe.

The sling was the simplest and least costly missile-throwing weapon. Made of leather or cloth, it had two thongs and was loaded with a small rock or lead shot. It was swung around until it reached the proper momentum when one of the thongs was released to fire the missile. A sling-thrown rock could penetrate the skin or even break bones. Larger versions of the sling were called fustibals. Attached to a wooden stick, the fustibal could launch larger missiles, including stinkpots full of burning sulphur or quicklime.

BELOW: **A list of English archers by order. Archery played an increasingly important role during the Crusade period.**

101

CHAPTER 7

Knightly Brotherhoods & Holy War

The First Crusade was the only one of nine military excursions to the Holy Land that achieved significant victories. Those that followed were, in effect, a series of campaigns to recoup losses suffered by the knights who had stayed behind to establish fiefdoms in the Christian Kingdom of Jerusalem. Since most crusading knights returned home with their victories and plunder after the First Crusade, the need to provide military protection to the new kingdom in the Holy Land became a critical issue.

The religious fervor of some Crusaders who stayed behind proved strong enough to inspire a new form of religious knighthood based in the Holy Land. These knights formed communities of monks and lay brothers who dressed alike in robes emblazoned with crosses and lived a uniform communal life. The two most important of these orders were the Knights Templars, consisting mainly of English knights, and the Knights Hospitallers, whose numbers came primarily from England and Italy. Leading to the formation of many other secular brotherhoods of knights in Europe, the Knights Templars and the Knights Hospitallers became two of the earliest international military forces.

BELOW: A community of monks and lay brothers tending the sick in Jerusalem.

OPPOSITE: Interior of the Temple Church, a Norman round church founded in London in 1185, which formed part of the seat of the Knights Templars in England.

The process started in the foundation of a non-military institution, the Hospital of St. John the Compassionate. The increased influx of pilgrims into Jerusalem created a need for a place to house those who had been injured en route, who had suffered from sicknesses contracted along the way or who simply had impoverished themselves during their travels. Benedictine monks first began operating a hospital in Jerusalem for Christian pilgrims in 1070. A group of merchants from Amalfi, Italy, had set up the hospital with the understanding that it was the site of the Latin Hospice originally founded in Jerusalem by Charlemagne. Separate hospitals probably existed for men and women, and women were affiliated with the order as well as men.

After the Crusaders' 1099 victory, the work of the Hospital of St. John expanded rapidly. Wealthy European knights began making substantial donations to aid the work of the Hospital. Godfred of Boulogne and Baldwin I were among the many honorary members, called donats, who created an endowment for this altruistic institution through donations of land in both Europe and the Holy Land. The monks who ran the Hospital quickly developed a reputation for serving Christian pilgrims wine and bread, while they themselves partook of water and lesser fare.

The Knights Templars

While traveling overland through the Byzantine Empire, pilgrims from Western Europe were often attacked by roving bands of Moslems, or Saracens as they were called then. Inspired by the success of the Hospitallers of St. John, religiously inclined knights founded a second brotherhood in 1118 and called themselves the Knights Templars. This organization patrolled the road to Jerusalem and protected pilgrims. The Templars represented a new union of religious orders of knighthood with military service. Known as the Knights of the Red Cross, which served as their insignia, they became the first and most powerful of many similar brotherhoods to follow.

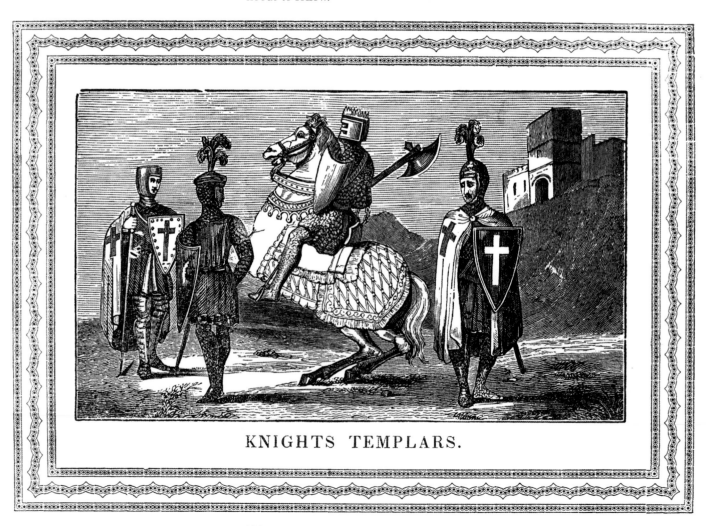

KNIGHTS TEMPLARS.

Their founder Hugh de Payens, a Frankish knight from Burgundy, and Godfrey of St. Omer, another one of the original members of the Knights Templars, had both won recognition for their bravery during the First Crusade. They traveled to Rome with four other knights to seek recognition from the Church. The fledgling organization they helped start was given space in a building near the Dome of the Rock in Jerusalem. One of Islam's most sacred spots, the Dome was important in Christianity as the site of the Temple of Solomon. Its designation as a temple gave the Templars their name. They were also known as the Knights of the Temple of Solomon and the Poor Knights of Christ. The nine founding knights took vows of poverty, chastity and obedience, and the order adopted the Benedictine rule, which emphasized work and moderation rather than monastic austerity. In the past, the Church had relied on excommunication or interdicts to enforce its laws and exert its power. Now it had its first real army.

From its original mission to protect pilgrims traveling to Jerusalem, the Knights Templars soon expanded to include general fighting against "infidels" by 1140. Donations to the order from European knights became an alternative to fighting in the Holy Land and a way of aligning oneself with a holy cause. Count Fulk of Anjou was one of the knights who began to worry about his soul after warring with the King of England. In 1120, he traveled to Jerusalem as a pilgrim and joined the Knights Templars. Representatives of the Church in the new Christian state of Jerusalem made generous donations and supported their activities. Married knights were allowed to join the Templars for life or a set term, once they committed half their property to the order. They were not, however, allowed to wear the Templars' white robe and red cross.

In the meantime, the Knights Hospitallers also expanded their operations to include military service. The Friars of the Hospital of St. John of Jerusalem became a separate order attached to the Knights Hospitallers, gaining official recognition from Pope Paschall II in 1113. Under the leadership of Raymond du Puy, the new order followed the model of military service provided by the Knights Templars. Four categories of the new Hospitallers existed: knights of justice, who came from the nobility and had already been dubbed knights; chaplains, who met the spiritual needs of the order; serving brothers, who did much of the work; and donats, who were honorary members giving money and estates. The financial success of the Hospitallers quickly led to the establishment of subsidiary preceptories throughout Europe. They became known as Knights of the White Cross because of their red military gowns with white crosses. Both they and the Knights Templars played significant roles in the Crusades that followed the first one in 1099.

ABOVE: **A German Templar knight. The organization took its name from the Temple of Solomon in Jerusalem, near which it occupied space.**

ABOVE: An illuminated manuscript of William of Tyre, written in about 1250, depicts the army of Saladin ravaging the Holy Land.

BELOW RIGHT: A procession of monks led by St. Bernard takes over the Cistercian monastery at Clairvaux in France. Distinguished for his unusual eloquence, he preached the Second Crusade.

The Second Crusade

The first Crusader siege of Jerusalem was followed within a month by a battle in nearby Ascalon against Moslem forces who had come up from Egypt. The Crusaders used the element of surprise to win a decisive victory there, and a period of relative peace followed in the Holy Land. The knightly brotherhoods and princes of Jerusalem concentrated on fortification of the coastal region and the building of castles to act as bases of operation for Christian knights. Control of the high seas grew increasingly important. Despite the establishment of the Knights Hospitallers and the Knights Templars, peace was not to be permanent.

The Second Crusade (1147-1149) was sparked by the fall of Edessa to Turkish Moslems in 1144. The charismatic preaching of St. Bernard of Clairvaux in Europe inspired Emperor Conrad III of Germany and King Louis VII of France to take their armies to the Holy Land. They traveled separately through the Balkans, pillaging parts of the Byzantine Empire as they went, and crossed into Asia Minor with help from the Byzantine Emperor Manuel I, who was happy to be rid of them. Conrad's forces were decimated outside the Turkish city Dorylaeum in an ambush by Turkish Moslems. After the remains of his army joined forces with King Louis at the Palestinian port city of Acre, the Crusaders marched to Damascus, where they were roundly defeated. The Latin princes of the Kingdom of Jerusalem failed to support their efforts, but the Knights Templars helped reorganize Crusader forces

and get them to the coast. Both Conrad and Louis returned home without victory.

In 1154 Ascalon once again became the site of conflict with Saracens, and the Hospitallers joined forces with the Knights Templars to recapture the city, followed by another period of relative peace in the Holy Land. By 1187, however, Moslem forces had become active again. Jerusalem fell into Saracen hands. The Hospitallers withdrew from the city and established themselves at Margat, a fortified town north of Jerusalem in the principality of Antioch. From Rome, Pope Gregory VIII issued the call for the Third Crusade (1189-1192).

Saladin Unites the Moslems

The great Kurdish warrior Saladin, Sultan of Egypt, was the Saracen military leader responsible for the loss of Jerusalem to Moslem forces. His military expertise was aided by recurrent squabbling among the Christian princes in the Holy Land and knights who arrived on Crusade. Uniting the warring Saracen tribes in a jihad, or Moslem holy war, Saladin captured Damascus in Syria and went on to take the rest of Syria and Palestine. He then formed an alliance with Raymond of Tripoli, but

ABOVE: **Louis VII of France, Emperor Conrad III of Germany, and Baldwin III, Latin king of Jerusalem, meet to discuss the state of the Second Crusade.**

the Christian knight shifted his loyalties back to the Crusaders. Saladin defeated them at Hattin, near the Sea of Galilee in what is now Israel, with 30,000 soldiers including 12,000 cavalry. Two prominent knights, Guy de Lusignan and Reynald de Chatillon, were captured among others. Chatillon was executed, and Lusignan, former regent of Jerusalem, won his freedom by persuading the forces at Ascalon to surrender.

Three Western European leaders took up the call and marched to the Holy Land: King Richard I of England, King Philip II of France and German Emperor Frederick Barbarossa. Frederick arrived first, but Byzantine Emperor Isaac II threw in his lot with Saladin and Frederick had to fight his way to the Bosporus Sea. He sacked Adrianople and forced the Greeks to provide his army with transportation to Asia Minor. Before ever reaching the Holy City, Frederick drowned in the Goksu River in Cilicia or Little Armenia — now part of Turkey — and his army dispersed.

Richard and Philip landed at Acre in 1189. Once secured by the Crusaders, Acre became the new base of operation for the Knights Hospitallers. Jerusalem had already been under attack for two years, the siege prolonged by feuding between Guy of Lusignan and Conrad, Marquis of Montferrat, over which of them would rule the city once it was captured. By 1191 Jerusalem fell to the Christians, its remaining citizens on the verge of starvation. The victory was far from decisive. Philip returned home, but Richard marched to Jaffa and built a fortification there. He also rebuilt Ascalon, which had been razed by the Saracens.

In an 1192 truce with Saladin, the Christians retained Jaffa and access to the Holy Sepulchre — all that remained of the Kingdom of Jerusalem. Antioch and Tripoli also remained in Christian hands, and Richard gave Cyprus, which he had conquered en route, to Guy de Lusignan. What little was gained by the Third Crusade came about because of Richard's skill at negotiation and Saladin's willingness to compromise. Richard returned to England without recapturing Jerusalem in 1191, and Saladin died the following year. The next hundred years in the Holy Land were marred by intense rivalry between the Knights Hospitallers and the Knights Templars.

Opportunism & Idealism

The Fourth Crusade (1202-1204) got sidetracked by political intrigues. Led by the French preacher Fulk of Neuilly, crusading knights gathered outside of Venice, but many of them lacked the funds to pay for ship passage to Palestine. The Venetian doge, Enrico Dandolo, hired them to march to Dalmatia, now Croatia, where they recovered the city of Zara from the Hungarians and sacked it. Censure by the Pope

ABOVE: **Richard I unhorsing Saladin, the Sultan of Egypt, during the Third Crusade.**

OPPOSITE: **Richard I leading Crusaders against the Moslems at Acre.**

did little to end Crusader entanglements in such political embroglios. They next invaded Constantinople, deposed Byzantine Emperor Alexius III and pillaged the city for the doge, who led their forces despite his age and blindness. In the wake of more political upheaval, the Latin Empire of Constantinople was formed. It was the first time the capital of the Byzantine Empire had fallen in 800 years. The splendorous wealth of what had been the greatest European city of the Middle Ages was divided among the crusading knights and their Venetian supporters. The Greeks recaptured Constantinople in 1261.

Disillusion with the opportunism and greed of their elders during the Fourth Crusade may have provided the impetus for thousands of French children who left on the Children's Crusade in 1212. Their mission had a tragic outcome. Departing in ships from Marseilles, they were sold into slavery by the ships' captains. A contingent of German children, which traveled overland, was all but annihilated by hunger and disease.

The Fifth – Eighth Crusades

The target of the Fifth Crusade (1217-1221) was Egypt, seat of Saracen power and the key to recovery of the Holy Land. Led by King Andrew II of Hungary, Duke Leopold VI of Austria and John of Brienne, crusading knights won the Egyptian city of Damietta despite a chain spanning the Nile River there. Soon after, they had

to return the city to win their freedom when they were defeated at Cairo.

No fighting took place at the start of the Sixth Crusade (1228-1229) during which Emperor Frederick II of Germany made a truce with Saracen leaders. Part of Jerusalem and a number of holy sites were returned temporarily to Christian hands. When the Saracens reoccupied Jerusalem, though, Thibault IV of Navarre in Spain, the count of Champagne and Richard of Cornwall resumed hostilities. They were hampered by a political dispute between the Knights Hospitallers and the Knights Templars over which Moslem faction to ally with. It had become clear that there would be no victory without such an alliance. The Knights Templars succeeded in convincing the Crusaders to support the sultan of Damascus rather than to ally with Egyptian Moslems. A 1244 treaty with Damascus restored Palestine to Christian hands. That same year, the Mamluks, Egyptian slaves who had risen to positions of power, captured Jerusalem and defeated the Crusaders decisively at Gaza.

King Louis IX of France, also called Saint Louis, headed the efforts to restore Jerusalem to Christianity during the Seventh Crusade (1248-1254). Crusader forces once more concentrated their campaigns in Egypt, recapturing Damietta in 1249 but once again failing to defeat Moslem forces at Cairo. Saint Louis himself was captured and had to buy his freedom. After his release, he spent four years rebuilding the Holy Land castles and fortifications that remained in Christian hands. It was probably his most important contribution to the Crusade effort. The Eighth Crusade (1270) was again led by Saint Louis. The unlikely target was Tunis, chosen by Louis's brother Charles of Anjou to enhance his holdings in Sicily. The Crusaders were stricken by disease and the campaign was aborted by Saint Louis's death.

The Last Holy Land Crusade

Motivated by the fall of Jaffa and Antioch, the last of the great advances on the Holy Land by Christian knights resulted in the Ninth Crusade (1271-1272). Prince Edward, later King of England, landed at Acre and withdrew after negotiating a truce. Tripoli fell into Saracen hands in 1289, and the last Christian outpost in the Holy Land, Acre, was lost in 1291.

The Knights Hospitallers withdrew from the Holy Land after the fall of Acre and established themselves on the island of Cyprus. They continued to wage their fight against the Saracens, but primarily by sea rather than on land. The first appointment of a Hospitallers' Admiral of the Galleys came in 1299. As well as impeding piracy, the Hospitallers became the conduit to the Holy Land for Christian pilgrims. Deciding that the Greek island of Rhodes was a more strategic site for their operations, the Hospitallers' grand master William de Villaret ousted

ABOVE: **Louis IX leading soldiers of the Seventh Crusade in Egypt shortly before his own capture at Al- Mansüra on February 8, 1250.**

ABOVE: **Emperor Charles V, shown with symbols of the Holy Roman Empire, granted the Mediterranean island of Malta to the wandering Knights of Rhodes in 1530.**

BELOW: **Philip IV, King of France, together with Edward II of England, supported persecution of the Knights Templars beginning in 1308.**

its Saracen occupants in 1310 with help from his brother Fulk de Villaret. Once established on Rhodes, the Hospitallers became known as the Knights of Rhodes. Aided by the king of Cyprus, they briefly captured the city of Alexandria in 1365. In the 16th century, they bravely defended themselves against an onslaught by Turkish Moslems until 1522, when they were ejected from the island. They wandered homeless until Emperor Charles V gave them the Mediterranean island of Malta, after which they became known as the Knights of Malta. After fortifying the island, they successfully defended it against Turkish Moslems in 1565. Although they still exist as a charitable organization committed to care of the sick and disabled, the Knights Hospitallers were ejected from Malta by Napoleon in 1798 and never again wielded the same prominence and power.

The Knights Templars met a more tragic end. From the beginning, the Templars were accused — often unfairly — of conspiring with the enemy to advance themselves. After securing the throne of Jerusalem for Guy of Lusignan and his consort Sibylla, they were forced out of Jerusalem when it was captured by Saladin. They moved to Acre once it was in Christian hands and followed the Hospitallers to Cyprus after Acre fell to the Saracens. By the 12th century, their great wealth motivated them to take up banking and money lending. The grandeur of their establishments in England and France subjected them to envy, particularly from King Philip IV of France. The Templars' worldliness and special privileges — they were accountable only to the Pope — also drew resentment from other secular clergymen. In need of money and coveting the Templars' holdings, Philip supported their persecution beginning in 1308. Seizing on the accusations of a Templar turncoat, Philip arrested the knights and forced confessions out of them by torture. In 1314, the last grand master, Jacques de Molay was burned at the stake. Fifty-four knights preceded him in 1310. The Order of the Poor Knights of the Temple of Solomon came to an end, and their property, earmarked for the Knights Hospitallers, mostly lined the pockets of Philip and his co-conspirator Edward II of England.

Results of the Crusades

Other Crusades to the Holy Land were preached, but none was actually under-
taken. During the period of the Crusades, the notion of a Crusade was used for
any campaign against infidels or heretics that had been sanctioned by the Pope.
While the Crusades to the Holy Land never succeeded at converting the region to
Christianity, they made other important contributions. Some of the barriers that
existed between Christian and Moslem cultures were eliminated. Trade increased,
and the Moslem world stopped being uncharted territory for Western Europeans.
Thanks to the Crusades, stories of noble knightly exploits multiplied, and the code
of chivalry reached an apogee. Many of the great castles built by crusading knights
in the Holy Land still stand as monuments to the glories of knighthood's campaigns
there. Venice and the other Italian port cities increased in wealth and prominence
as a result of aiding and transporting knights to the Holy Land, and the power of
the Pope was greatly enhanced by the leadership role he played in the holy wars
of knighthood. The two great religious orders of knighthood founded during the
Crusades — the Knights Hospitallers and the Knights Templars — did not always

ABOVE: **The Castle of the Grand Masters on the Greek island of Rhodes, where the Knights Hospitallers were reestablished in 1310 and became known as the Knights of Rhodes.**

ABOVE: **The burning of Knights**
Templars in 1310 by Philip IV
of France. Their leader Jacques
de Molay followed them to the
stake in 1314.

live up to the high standards they set for themselves. Accusations were often made of their debauchery and licentiousness. Their legacy was nevertheless one of idealistic commitment to military prowess in the cause of Christianity and for protection of the less powerful.

The Teutonic Knights

The third major religious order of knighthood in operation during the Crusade period was the Teutonic Knights. The brotherhood had its origins in a hospital founded at Acre for German knights set up in a beached boat during the Third Crusade by German merchants from the Hanseatic cities. The Teutonic Knights were modeled after the Knights Hospitallers and Knights Templars and took vows of poverty, chastity and obedience. Pope Clement III confirmed their formation in 1191 as a military order officially called the Brothers of the Hospital of St. Mary of the German Nation. Another lesser military order of knighthood founded during the Third Crusade was that of St. Thomas of Acre.

Early in the 13th century, the Teutonic Knights moved their base to Eastern Europe. After Andrew II of Hungary gave them Burzenland north of the Transylvanian Alps, they rose to fame as fighters of holy wars at home. The Teutonic Knights wore military gowns with a black cross. They had branches in Germany, Latvia and Prussia. Unlike most of the other orders of knighthood, the Teutonic Knights accepted individuals who had not already been knighted, although they followed the precepts of the religious orders of knighthood in most other ways.

From 1221 to 1224, the Teutonic Knights fought against the Cumans, a

ABOVE: **A German knight of the Teutonic Knights, a military order officially formed as the Brothers of the Hospital of St. Mary.**

BELOW LEFT: **Knights of the Bath, from the 17th-century facsimile of the *Writhe's Garter* book. Knights of the Bath was not a specific brotherhood but a designation that the warrior had been dubbed in a special, often religious, ceremony.**

In this pajent is shewed howe the noble Erle Richard was made knyght of the Garter at that tyme to his great worship. And after by marvaill actt by hym ful notabli and knyghtili acheved in his pere psone. Did greet honor & worship to the noble order of knyghtes of the Garter. as by the pajent hereafter folowyng more pleynly is shewed.

nomadic Turkish tribe, in Transylvania. They next crusaded against heathen Prussians in 1226 for Duke Conrad of Masovia, now part of Poland. As a result of their successes they were granted special privileges and the lands they conquered from pagan tribes. They formed an independent state in Prussia, now part of Germany. Over a period of 50 years, the Teutonic Knights gradually subdued the rest of what was then Prussia.

Formation of knightly orders grew popular in Germany, and there were many configurations of them. In 1237, the Teutonic Knights absorbed the Livonian Knights, a religious order of knighthood founded by the Latvian bishop of Riga in 1202 to convert the Baltic countries. A defeat by Latvian forces motivated the Livonian Knights, also called the Brothers of the Sword, to joined with the Teutonic Knights. They regained their independence once the secularization of the Teutonic Knights took place in 1525. The Prussian order of Dobrin was also absorbed by the Teutonic Knights. By 1279 their numbers had grown to over 2,000.

The seat of operations for the Teutonic Knights was Marienburg, now situated in Poland. The Knights colonized Prussia with German settlers, and campaigned regularly in Lithuania as well as Prussia. They were closely linked with German Emperor Frederick II. After the Pope granted them trading privileges, the Teutonic Knights drifted away from crusading to more politically motivated skirmishes and commercial enterprises. A defeat in battle against the Poles in 1410 at Tannenburg left the Teutonic Knights in disarray. By 1466, the Peace of Thorun subjected them to Polish authority. During the Reformation their grand master Albert of Brandenburg secularized Prussia, and the Teutonic Knights lost what little power they still had.

The Spanish Orders of Knighthood

Spain provided the locus for yet another series of military orders of knighthood. By the middle of the 12th century, European divisions of both the Knights Templars and the Knights Hospitallers had taken up the cause of the Reconquest, as the return of Spain to Christian control was called. Following their example, a number of local military orders sprang up. The oldest of them, the Order of Calatrava, was started in Castile in 1156 to protect Toledo and the route south. Their name came from their mission to defend the plains of Calatrava, which had been captured from the Moors in 1146. The Pope confirmed their formation as a military order in 1164. A separate Castilian order of the Knights of Calatrava, called the Knights of Aviz, was formed in what is now Portugal.

The order of Alcantara was established to defend a castle in Calatrava captured from the Moors. Originally called the Knights of St. Julian, they were founded around 1156 and their order confirmed by the Pope in 1177. The order of Santiago — formally the Knights of St. James of Compostela — began in Léon in 1170 and was confirmed in 1175. The smaller order of Montegaudio, based primarily in Aragon, was founded three years later by a disaffected member of the order of Santiago. It

eventually joined with the Hospital of the Holy Redeemer at Teruel and with the Knights Templars and concentrated on ransoming Christian captives. Two more orders, San Jorge de Alfama and Santa Maria de Espana, were set up at the end of the 12th century and the beginning of the 13th century, while the order of Montesa was started to defend the border in Murcia.

Secular Orders of Knighthood

Part of the legacy of the military orders of knighthood was the foundation of secular brotherhoods in the 14th and 15th centuries, such as the orders of the Garter and the Thistle in England and the order of the Golden Fleece in France. The most famous of them were started by the princes of Europe's knighthood, and these orders were characterized by elaborate ceremonial rituals and dress regulations. The oldest of them was the Order of the Band, founded by King Alfonso XI of Castile in 1330. The Order of the Garter, started by King Edward III of England, began in 1348. According to a probably apocryphal story, the countess of Salisbury lost her garter, and it was returned by a gallant knight. When he said, *"Honi soit qui mal y pense* (Evil to him who thinks it evil),"* he supplied the order with its famous motto.

Other secular orders of chivalry included: the Order of the Star, founded in 1351 by King John of France; the Order of the Knot, started by Louis of Naples in 1352; the Order of the Golden Buckle, begun by German Emperor Charles IV in 1355; the Order of the Sword, instituted by King Peter of Cyprus in 1359; the Order of the Collar, organized by the Count of Savoy in 1363; the Order of the Dragon, founded by German Emperor Sigismund around 1413; the Order of the Golden Fleece, started by Philip the Good, Duke of Burgundy, in 1431; the Order of the Swan, begun by Brandenburg Duke Albert Achilles in 1444; the Order of the Croissant, instituted by René of Anjou in 1448 and the Order of St. Michael, organized by French King Louis XI in 1469. Brotherhoods started by lesser knights include the Order of Fools, 1331; the Confraternity of the Black Swan, 1352; and the Order of the Golden Apple, 1390.

The lay confraternities had no specific religious mission and were not subject to ecclesiastical authority, but they often contained a charitable or religious element. Saying masses for the dead, providing education and caring for the old and infirm were suitable secular order activities. The orders often adopted a patron saint and held special celebrations on feast days. St. George was the patron for the Order of the Garter, St. Maurice served as the patron for the Order of the Croissant and the Holy Spirit served for the Order of the Knot. In some cases, lay orders provided funds for Crusades or aided in the recruitment of knights for Crusades.

Politics or diplomacy might also motivate the formation of confraternities, as was the case for the Order of the Garter. Through its establishment, King Edward III of England hoped to legitimize his war against the King of France. The proliferation of orders of knighthood in Germany can be ascribed to the power vacuum created by the decline of the empire's power there. Secular orders served as a means of unifying knights in a particular region, and their statutes could forbid members from joining any other such societies.

Tournament societies rather than the military orders may have been equally responsible for inspiring formation of the secular societies of knighthood. The rules for the Castilian Order of the Band included components typical for tourneying societies, and the seating for members of the Order of the Garter in St. George's Chapel may reflect the makeup of tournament teams.

BELOW: **To settle troubles in Ireland, Richard II knighted four native kings in 1395 in an attempt at conciliation.**

CHAPTER 8

Tournaments, Jousts & Heraldry

Much like football and other spectator sporting events in the modern world, tournaments served as festive and colorful occasions, full of pageantry. These public contests between knights flourished from the 12th to the 16th century. As social events and valuable training for knighthood, they probably exerted a more important influence on Medieval life than even the Crusades. The medieval tournament epitomized the ideals represented by the code of chivalry. In tournaments, or tourneys as they were also called, knights divided themselves into teams that were led by champions. As many as 3,000 knights might participate in a single tournament.

The joust was the form of military contest that occurred between single opponents and might be held separately or as part of a tourney. In their heyday, tournaments were as elaborate as theatrical events, often planned on the occasion of a marriage, a coronation or a diplomatic mission. Manuals elaborately detailed their intricate rules and regulations.

The origin of tournaments and jousts can be traced to trials by combat, which served as a means of resolving disputes in the Middle Ages. An even earlier precedent can be found in the gladiatorial contests of Roman days. In the ninth century Frankish rulers instituted an early form of tourney when they reviewed cavalry maneuvers. From its origins in the Frankish territories, tournaments and jousting spread into Germany, England and southern Europe. The regulations governing them followed their dissemination and became universal.

The organizers of tournaments were usually kings or other nobles. At least several weeks in advance, the announcement of a tournament went out, delivered by messengers. The knights invited to participate gathered with an entourage and camped near the tournament fields. They hung their armorial insignia outside of their tents or in the windows of their rooms if they were staying in a town. They might also display them outside castles, monasteries or other public places. The purpose was to give anyone who had a complaint against them an opportunity to announce it,

BELOW: Armorial Bearings of the Macdougal family. Such heraldic devices identified knights and encapsulated family history.

OPPOSITE: An illustration of knights arriving at a tournament, from a 15th-century work on tourneys by René d'Anjou.

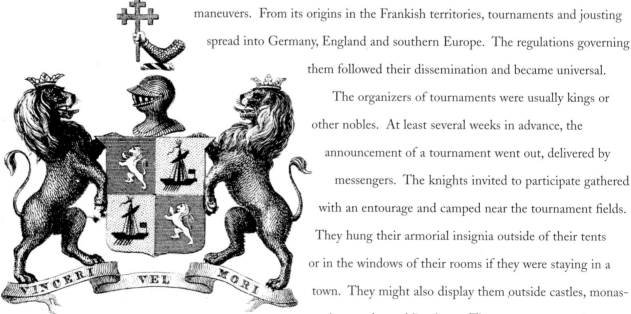

ABOVE: **Ceremony at the start of a tournament, from the 15th-century illuminated manuscript of René d'Anjou. Different types of armor and weaponry are visible.**

which if valid created a blot on the knight's scutcheon, or shield. A knight "without reproach" had no blots on his scutcheon. Lists of the reproaches that could bar a knight from a tournament included excommunication, slander of women, murder, lying, fugitive status and arson. The public display of coats of arms discouraged robber knights from participating in the events. Eventually, hereditary qualification — proof of at least four generations of knighthood — became a way of limiting tournaments to the nobility.

In the days preceding the event, horse traders arrived on site to equip knights in need of a mount, clothiers offered wares for both combatants and their horses, and moneylenders struck deals in case of ransom. A ragtag band of fortune tellers, mimes, acrobats, minstrels, troubadours and poets, as well as women of high and low repute, collected. Dancing, gambling and other diversions marked the occasion, which might also precipitate a fight or two.

The Tournament

The fields, called lists, were oval or rectangular and demarcated by barriers. They could be set up within a town square or in the countryside. Pavilions were constructed along the barriers for important spectators, including judges and ladies who

122

sponsored particular knights. Balconies, festooned with tapestries, pennants and coats of arms, housed the wealthiest spectators, who tossed coins into the crowd below them in acts of generosity. After the qualifications of the participating knights had been reviewed by the judges, a herald called off their names, and they entered the lists in full armor, with their horses caparisoned, or outfitted in ornamental trappings.

The program for a tournament consisted of a series of events, lasting a day or up to a week. Individual jousting matches were part of the activities and might be preceded or followed up by mock battles, called melees, between teams of knights. The judges or a Queen of Beauty, selected specially for the tournament, awarded prizes to the winning knights. Contestants used the tourney to demonstrate their military prowess and bravery. A newly dubbed knight could build up his reputation by participating in tournaments and make a substantial income from ransoms and prizes. A knight sometimes planned strategy or acted as a bodyguard for another knight of higher rank. Boys too young to participate organized their own contests in imitation.

A Mirror of Warfare

Tournaments mirrored real war as much as possible. Tactics and ruses were important. Claiming to be observers, a group of knights might enter the fray at the last minute when the other team had exhausted themselves in fighting. Nothing prevented a group of knights from accosting a solitary contestant or one knight from taking a wounded combatant prisoner. The legendary William Marshal once came upon a knight who had fallen during a tournament and broken his leg. Marshal

ABOVE: **Portrait of Antoine, Grand Batard de Bourgogne, by Roger van der Weyden (1464). Antoine was a Marshal of the Lists, and the white arrow he carried could be thrown down before the combatants as a signal to stop fighting.**

BELOW LEFT: **Two knights tilting. Each has broken his lance against the other. The tilt, a fence running down the center of the list, prevented collisions between opposing horses and knights.**

dragged him to a nearby inn, offered him to a group of his friends who were dining and said, "Take him to pay your debt." In addition to the seasoning that the martial practice of tournaments offered, they taught newly dubbed knights how to fight as a group.

Defeated knights gave their parole, or word of honor, and paid a ransom. They were also expected to part with their horses, weapons and armor as booty. Contestants started from refuges at either end of the lists. Racing at full gallop, they attempted to unhorse their opponents with their couched lances. Once a knight was unhorsed, the rules required that his opponent also dismount. Then the opponents continued to fight on the ground with swords and maces. The contest continued until one of the combatants cried "Quits" or was declared hors de combat — eliminated — from injury, fatigue or death. Judges or sponsors might also end a contest. In the early days, a tournament could range across the countryside, with designated refuges where knights could rest or rearm themselves. Occasionally, tournaments included contests on foot. Then knights wore field harness — battle armor — and used swords, axes, maces and poleaxes, or short-handled battle axes. A general mêlée of knights fighting on foot served as a popular way to end a tournament.

As tournaments evolved, the contest was fought on a single field, and knights were limited to a certain number of charges. Tournament fighting ended at dusk, when the knights gathered to collect their prizes and negotiate over ransoms. Honor played an important role in tournaments, so much so that a knight who won most of the prizes might turn them over to others as an act of generosity. At

ABOVE: **A mock battle, or mêlée, between teams of knights mirrored real war.**

times tournaments became pretexts for settling scores or resolving political disputes and personal rivalries. When William de Valence was beaten up by his opponent's squires at a Newbury, England, tournament in 1248, he returned the favor during a contest at Brackley the same year.

The contests were particularly risky when real weapons were used, and many knights were killed or seriously injured during tournaments. Geoffrey de Mandeville was trampled to death at a tournament in 1216. Sixty to 80 knights died during a tournament at Neuss, Germany, in 1240, many of them suffocating to death from the heat and dust. In 1350, when the Combat of the Thirty was fought in Brittany, the winning French team lost three knights. Twelve members of the losing team of Englishmen and Bretons died in the contest, and every one of the survivors was injured. To make the contests less dangerous, the practice of erecting a barrier, or tilt, was started in the 15th century in Italy. Initially it consisted of cloth hung over a rope, but in time a five-to-six-foot wooden fence running down the center of the list was used. It prevented opposing horses and knights from colliding.

Once tournaments became well established, the knights usually fought with blunted, or rebated, lances, swords and maces. Weapons specifically designed for use

BELOW: **A manuscript illumination of the jousts of St. Ingelbert near Calais in 1390. The artist included a tilt barrier for the combatants, but this in fact was not used in tournaments of the 14th century.**

in tournaments were developed in the middle of the 13th century, and a contest with blunted weapons was called a joust à plaisance, or joust of peace. A royal tournament held at Windsor in 1278 used leather armor and swords with whale-bone blades. Rebated lances had coronels, which were crown-shaped iron heads, at the tips. For jousts à outrance, or jousts of war, sharpened weapons were the rule, although even sharpened lances used in tournament combat might have blunted points.

A Shift Towards Masculine Display

The growth in tournaments marked a shift away from a culture of violence to one of masculine display. For the most part, women played a minor role in the world of the knight at war. At tournaments, though, women provided the inspiration for knights' feats of valor. A knight pledged himself to a lady he admired, and her presence spurred him on. Knights often made special vows dedicated to ladies they admired and carried their tokens — scarves, ribbons, veils or gloves — as talismen.

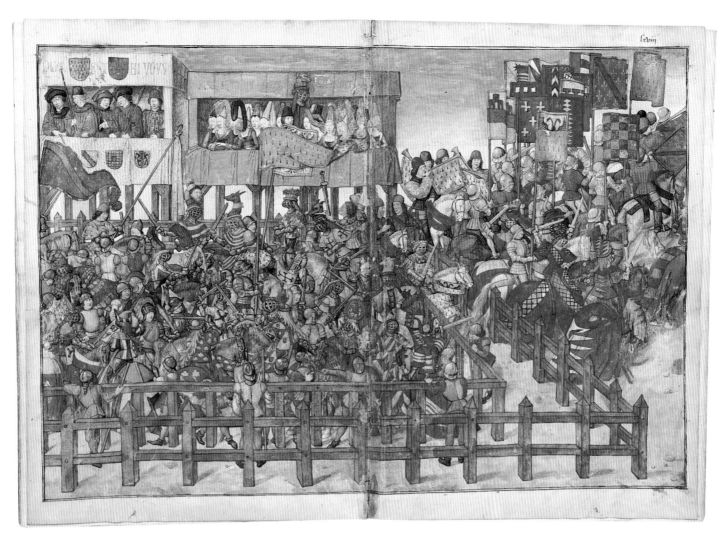

Mariolatry — the cult of the Virgin Mary — led to an idealization of women and promotion of feminine values that were related to the era's courtly love traditions. The poems and stories of the troubadours that celebrated feats of knighthood intertwined them with tales of idealized love that eroticized the bravery of knights. The connection between knighthood and courtly love is illustrated by the fact that those members of the nobility who patronized courtly literature were the ones who supported tournaments.

Banning Tournaments

Political leaders and the Church repeatedly called for the regulation or outright ban of tournaments and jousts, but their censure met with little success because of the games' great popularity. Political leaders frowned on tournaments because they depleted the supply of knights for political battles. They also gave rivals the occasion to stage rebellions. King Philip the Fair of France went so far as to ban all tournaments in 1312 to make sure the one he planned for his eldest son's knighting had no competition. Church disapproval was due in part to the adulterous undercurrents caused by the practice of knights pledging themselves to already married ladies. A knight's reward for winning in the lists was sometimes a kiss from his love.

Top: Illumination from the 15th-century work of René d'Anjou showing ladies watching a tournament.

Above: Pope John XXII in 1316 lifted the ban imposed on tournaments by Pope Innocent II in 1130.

127

ABOVE: **The Warwick shaffron, probably English from the second half of the 14th century, was plate armor shaped to enclose the horse's entire head.**

BELOW: **Helmets and visors of the 15th century for foot combat or the joust.**

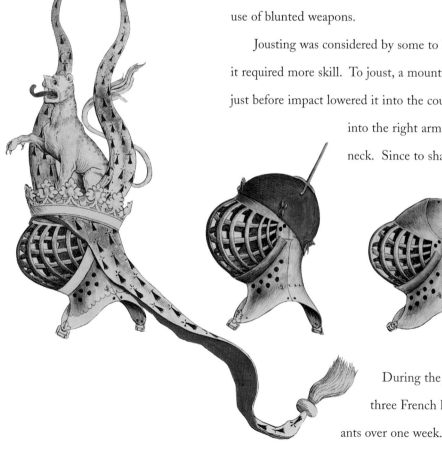

Condemning the promotion of violence in tournaments, Pope Innocent II banned them in 1130. Speaking at the Council of Clermont, he called them "those detestable markets and fairs, vulgarly called tournaments, at which knights are wont to assemble to order to display their strength and their rash boldness." Knights killed during tournaments were routinely denied a Christian burial, and the Archbishop of Saxony excommunicated all who participated in tournaments in 1175 after hearing that 16 knights had died jousting. According to the Church, such contests promoted all seven of the deadly sins. One knight protested that the Pope had removed his only means of supporting himself.

Pope John XXII lifted the ban, which had never been effective, in 1316. One reason for the ban's inefficacy lay in the association of tournaments with Christian ideals and, in particular, with crusading. One story circulated of a knight on his way to a tournament who stopped to pray to the Virgin. By the time he arrived at the lists, the competition had ended, but he was roundly applauded because the Virgin had appeared and competed for him. Knights who were injured or died at tournaments obviously could not participate in the Crusades. Yet tournaments also served as recruiting grounds for the Crusades. King Richard I legalized tournaments in England in 1194 and helped develop regulations for them. He licensed five jousting fields and levied fees on the participants, from earls through knights without property. King Edward I detailed the number of supporters a knight could bring, sanctioned grooms and footmen from carrying weapons, and required the use of blunted weapons.

Jousting was considered by some to be less dangerous than tourneys, although it required more skill. To joust, a mounted knight carried his lance raised, then just before impact lowered it into the couched position, which meant it was tucked into the right arm and pointed diagonally over the horse's neck. Since to shatter an opponent's lance won a knight points in the contest, hollow and jointed lances were used to create a more dramatic effect. A strike to the head counted more than one to the torso, and if a contestant hit his opponent's legs or horse, he would lose points.

During the jousts of St. Ingelbert near Calais in 1390, three French knights met 36 different foreign combatants over one week.

Tournament Armor

By the 14th century, special armor was designed for tournaments. Over time it became heavier — 100 pounds — than war armor, which averaged 60 pounds. The most common tournament headgear was the frog-mouthed helm, which was heavier than a contemporary war helmet and had a narrow eye slit. Placed high for protection, the eye slit gave the knight a view of his opponent only when he leaned forward in jousting position. It was often worn with a padded hood. Since a knight's left side took most of the blows, tournament armor was heavier or reinforced on that side. Broad surfaces were designed to deflect the lance blow away from the body.

A cuirass or chest armor for tournaments usually had a lance rest, and back armor was usually lightweight, at times no more than two crossed iron strips. A large gauntlet, called a manifer, covered the left hand and lower arm. A besagew, or circular plate, covered the right armpit, and a poldermitten reinforced the armor on the right arm. By the 15th century, shields were no longer used in warfare but only in tournaments. An innovation introduced in the 16th century, exchange pieces allowed a knight to convert his regular armor to tournament use. Garniture, as such accessories were called, allowed a knight to add and subtract as many as 20 or 30 related interchangeable armor pieces according to context and need.

BELOW: **Early 16th-century German knights clad in elaborate parade armor.**

Horses wore plate-armor shaffrons, or head pieces, that in some cases had no sights to prevent the animal from shying. In German tournaments, horses wore stechsacks, which were padded neck and chest defenses against lance blows. Tournament saddles lacked the high cantles of saddles used in real combat. One type of German tournament saddle positioned the knight almost a foot above the horse's back. Two curved wooden bars supported the rear of the knight's thighs and kept him in upright position. The front of the saddle rested behind the horse's withers like a fork and protected the fronts of the knight's legs.

ABOVE: **Richard I, the first king to adopt a heraldic device, carried a shield with two lions rampant.**

The Tournament as Pageantry

The pageantry of tournaments and jousts gradually took precedence over their function as a form of military practice. Costumes or disguises were popular, and knights sometimes dressed as monks, women, Romans and even cardinals. Reflecting the importance of chivalric literature's contribution, Arthurian legends created the models for many tournaments. One such event held in Cyprus in 1223 celebrated the knighting of the son of a Crusader, John of Ibelin, and featured a full cast of Arthurian characters played by attending knights and ladies. The Bavarian knight Ulrich von Lichtenstein toured the countryside dressed in Arthurian costume and welcomed all who defeated him in a joust to join him at the Round Table. An accomplished and reputable warrior, Ulrich also toured as Venus from Italy to Bohemia. Such pageantry reflected a growing sense of nostalgia for the bygone glory of knighthood.

Extravagant displays of tournament pageantry served as a means of plowing back into the economy some of the wealth accumulated by the wealthiest members of the aristocracy. When the Duke of Burgundy married England's Princess Margaret, the accompanying tournament lasted 14 days. The contest was executed like a theatrical piece along the theme of a captive giant and a princess from a distant island. To win the tournament a knight had to free the giant, and his prize was the princess. A dwarf dressed in red and white satin led the giant into the list by a chain and tied him to a golden tree. Each day of the tournament offered a different series of jousts, and the final event was a mêlée with 25 knights on each side. At the banquet marking the end of the tournament, a female dwarf in a golden gown presented a daisy to the bride, and a 60-foot mechanical whale was paraded past the guests.

Toward the end of the era of knighthood, Henry VIII jousted at his own coronation, wearing tournament armor he had designed for himself. He spent the equivalent of building and outfitting an entire warship for a tournament at Westminster in 1511. An ardent tourney fan, the English king maintained permanent lists at Hampton Court, Westminster and Greenwich. Henry VIII's most elegant tournament was held in 1520 outside of Calais, during which he and French king Francis I jousted. King Henry's horse was caparisoned in gold trappings fringed with damask. King Francis's horse wore purple trappings with gold trim and embroidery made of raven plumes. The English knights all wore outfits of gold cloth with reddish brown velvet, while the French knights appeared in silver cloth with purple velvet. Wrestling and archery — by then an anachronism — were part of the entertainment.

Probably the most prodigal and theatrical display of all at a tournament took place during the Feast of the Pheasant at Lille, France, in 1454. Philip of Burgundy planned the extravaganza to mark his departure for Constantinople on Crusade. Dressed as the Swan Knight, Adolf of Cleves challenged all comers to a joust before the banquet. Among the spectacles were a statue of a child that urinated rose water. At the finale, a giant dressed as a Saracen led an elephant into the banquet hall. On the elephant's back rode a weeping lady, meant to symbolize the Church and its oppression by "infidels." Many of the knights present vowed not to wear armor, sleep in a bed or sit down to eat until they had bested the Turks. By the reign of Elizabeth I, jousting at tournaments had been almost entirely eclipsed by masquerades or allegories and displays of manège, or horsemanship.

Heralds & Heraldry

The science or art of heraldry, the hereditary use of charges or iconic devices arranged on a shield, developed in the 12th century as a part of tournaments. Heraldic devices cropped up in more than one Western European kingdom between the First and Second Crusades. Before the Third Crusade, King Henry II of England, King Philip II of France and Count Philip of Flanders agreed on consistent insignia for their troops: white crosses for the English, red ones for the French and green for the Flemish. Soldiers had always needed a means of identification on the battlefield, but during the Crusades the muster of knights who spoke many different languages necessitated a system of identification that was simple and universal. Since they were in effect disguised by heavy armor, knights began by wearing distinctive crests on top of their helms to facilitate recognition. But the development of heraldry stems from far more than just the need for identification on the battlefield or in the lists,

which was more effectively accomplished with flags. Pleasure in vivid colors and decoration, along with a growing pride in heritage, characterized this period of knighthood.

Shields were painted with identifying insignia, but could be lost or destroyed during battle. Once insignia were sewn or embroidered on surcoats and tunics, the term "coat of arms" came into existence. Coats of arms became widespread during the 13th century, and the earliest ones were plain stripes or crosses. Since early shields often had reinforcing bands of metal or hardened leather, their surfaces offered an obvious place for painting. The first English king to adopt a heraldic device was Richard I, who chose two rampant lions facing each other. He added a third lion in 1195 and placed them all on a field of red to create what is still the Royal Arms of England. In the 15th century, Richard III formed the College of Arms, which is still in existence.

Quartering & Charges

As family histories grew more complex, knights acquired more than one coat of arms. Separate insignia were joined or amended when a knight acquired additional insignia through marriage, acquisition of new property or honors. The process of taking elements from two different arms to create new insignia was called compounding, and it signified the acquisition of new estates as well as family lineage. Quartering became necessary after the joining of two families had taken place. Devised at the end of the 13th century, quartering allowed a knight to put all family insignia on the same shield, which was divided into four quarters. Paternal insignia went in the first and fourth quarters, with lesser insignia in the second and third.

The most important components of a coat of arms were the charges that appeared on a knight's shield. The name for the most common charges was Ordinaries, and they included the chief, a broad horizontal band across the center; the pale, a vertical band down the center; the bend, a diagonal band through the center; the chevron, two diagonal stripes ending at the center; the cross; and the saltire, two bands crossing diagonally in the center. The most common colors used in coats of arms were gules (red), azure (blue), sable (black), and vert (green). Other colors frequently used by knights were purpure (purple), tenn (orange), murrey (reddish-purple), or (gold), and argent (white). A fundamental convention of heraldry prevented the placement of a metal (or argent) on another metal or a color on another color. Arms might also be decorated with fur or other rare materials.

Animals made up the most common images used on coats of arms. Lions, dragons, deer, boars and birds were popular, along with plants such as the rose, the fleur-de-lys and the cinquefoil. Eventually symbols of battle or jousting grew popular. They included arrows, swords, horseshoes, spurs and sleeves. The description of a particular heraldic insignia was called a blazon and consisted of a precise sequence of identifying characteristics.

ABOVE: **Richard III, King of England (1483-85), created the College of Arms.**

BELOW LEFT: **A mounted knight carrying a shield and wearing a quilted, skirted doublet, or gambeson, both decorated with heraldic devices.**

ABOVE: **Three entwined snakes form the coat of arms of a Welsh prince.**

BELOW: **Illumination from a 13th-century manuscript depicts two jousting knights.**

Regulation of Coats of Arms

The constant rearranging of Arms led to a need for regulation to prevent their whimsical or unmerited use and to make them consistently readable. The need developed to interpret these early logos, and the science of heraldry came into existence. The list of typical icons grew long, and a terminology to describe them evolved. The likeliest explanation for why this new science was called heraldry comes out of tournament protocol. Heralds proclaimed the start of these knightly contests and called out the names of the contestants. They are thought to be the ones who developed the rules and regulations of heraldry that appeared by the 13th century. Bartolus de Saxoferrato wrote the first treatise on heraldry, and by the 14th century, treatises on heraldry were published regularly, usually by heralds. When two knights had a dispute over possession of the same coat of arms, it was arbitrated in a Court of Chivalry, an institution that still exists.

Regulations promulgated as early as the 14th century prevented knights from adopting a coat of arms unless they were granted it by a king, a senior herald or a King of Arms. Replicas of knights' insignia also functioned as seals and were used for vow-taking. The practice of canting — making a visual pun out of a knight's name — reflects knighthood's sense of humor. One of the most comical examples of canting came out of the insignia for a family named Rand, which meant turnip. An image of the vegetable served as his insignia.

In the early days of heraldry, heralds wandered in the itinerant bands who followed tournaments. By the end of the 13th century, they became attached to the retinue of particular lords and wore their insignia. Then their task was to identify the insignia of all the noble families in a particular region and to become familiar with those of their master's enemies. Heralds were experts in armory and ceremony, collected fees, kept broken armor and enjoyed safe passage during war. Part of their job was to record promotions to knighthood before and during battle, as well as to keep track of those who had distinguished themselves, been wounded or died. They

even served a diplomatic role by acting as messengers between warring parties, and might muster the troops for a battle.

At tournaments, the herald inspected arms and crests to ensure their accuracy or validity and kept score of blows given or received during the contest. Expected to be of service to gentlewomen, a herald kept a record of those who oppressed widows or maidens. He might also carry messages between lovers. A literary education was an important requirement of a herald, who needed to be familiar with the mythically established arms of historical figures of knighthood. An understanding of the symbolism of plants, animals and colors was also important.

In a society that depended on visual symbols far more than literary ones, heraldry served an important and colorful purpose. It identified knights, encapsulated their family histories and contributed to the overall pageantry of the tournament and the battlefield.

TOP LEFT: **The king's arms are displayed in a volume (dated 1516) of a work that attempted to codify the entire body of law.**

ABOVE: **A lion rampant forms a Welsh coat of arms.**

CHAPTER 9

Legendary Leaders, Celebrated Conflicts

Knighthood produced many legendary leaders and memorable military engagements. In an era when catalogues and systems served as important ways of creating order, new heroes and important battles were classified in terms of models from the past. The 12th century saw a general revival of interest in stories from antiquity and provided a repertoire of stock heroes and events drawn from Roman and Biblical times. By the 15th century, tournaments incorporated elaborate charades based on legendary heroes. Alexander, Caesar, Abraham, Gideon, David and Judas Maccabeus became prefigurations of medieval knights. The accomplishments of the Frankish leader Charlemagne provided a more contemporary model. The fame of King Arthur of England took on mythic proportions and wielded great influence over the behavior of knights.

BELOW: **Armored soldiers guard a sleeping king clutching the Holy Grail in a scene from** Histoire du Graal **by Robert de Borron.**

OPPOSITE: **A battle scene from a manuscript depicts an attempt to liberate the Holy Grail from the infidel.**

King Arthur and the Knights of the Round Table

King Arthur lived well before the flowering of knighthood. Little of a factual nature is known about him. He was first mentioned in a Welsh poem, *Gododdin*, written around 600 A.D. and his reputation as a mighty warrior spread quickly. Geoffrey of Monmouth, the 12th-century bishop who wrote a history of English kings, immortalized Arthur as the conqueror of Europe. Out of his sometimes

fanciful accounts of Arthur's exploits grew some of the greatest epic literature of the age. The knights who frequented Arthur's Round Table included Perceval, written about by Chrétien de Troyes, and as Parzival by Wolfram von Eschenbach; Tristan, written about by Gottfried von Strassburg in the original version of the Tristan and Isolde legend; and Gawain, celebrated in the anonymously written *Sir Gawain and the Green Knight.*

One of the most famous themes of Arthurian legend involved pursuit of the Holy Grail. This chalice, dish or cup symbolized the holy mission of all knights

"without reproach". Brought to England by St. Joseph of Arimathea, the Holy Grail was supposedly used at the Last Supper and had miraculous powers to heal and provide food. The stories of King Arthur spread throughout Europe in the songs of minstrels. Later versions included stories about other Arthurian knights and ladies who frequented the Round Table in Camelot: Galahad, Lancelot, Kay, Queen Guinevere and the Lady of the Lake. Arthurian legend has inspired countless retellings, the most well known of which are Thomas Malory's 15th-century *Morte d'Arthur*, Alfred Tennyson's 19th-century *Idylls of the King* and Mark Twain's 19th-century *Connecticut Yankee in King Arthur's Court*. Popular modern renditions include T. H. White's *The Once and Future King*, and John Steinbeck's *The Acts of King Arthur and his Noble Knights*.

Frederick Barbarossa & Richard Lion-Heart

During the 12th century two great military leaders who provided models of knighthood were Frederick I of Germany and Richard I of England. King Frederick I of Germany, known as Frederick Barbarossa or Red Beard, was crowned Emperor in 1155. Before his death during the Third Crusade, he won fame for pacifying Germany, establishing its modern boundaries and by subduing the rest of the Holy Roman Empire. In addition to his feats as a Crusader, Frederick set limits on papal power by refusing to accept that his empire was held in fief to the Pope. Instead he claimed that his powers came directly from God through his election by the German princes. He successfully invaded Italy several times to reinforce his authority as a leader but then was defeated, first when his army was decimated in an epidemic outside of Rome and later by the Lombard League.

The feats of King Richard I, known as Richard Lion-Heart, during the Third Crusade won him laurels as the most famous crusading knight. He spent almost as much time in Europe — his mother was Eleanor of Aquitaine

— as he did in England, and he fought numerous wars there. Richard went to war twice against his father, King Henry II, the first time when he was 16. His role in extending the Angevin Empire started by his father was equal in importance to his accomplishments during the Third Crusade. Capitalizing on his travels in the Holy Land, Richard built Château Gaillard in France, basing it on an Islamic-influenced design. It remains the foremost example of military fortification constructed during the Middle Ages. En route home from Jerusalem, Richard was captured by Leopold II of Austria and ransomed by his own subjects. He returned briefly to England to put down a revolt against him. He died later in France in a minor skirmish.

William Marshal

Not all the great knights of the Middle Ages were born into positions of leadership like Frederick Barbarossa and Richard Lion-Heart. William Marshal offers an example of the upward mobility that a talented and lucky knight might achieve at the end of the 12th century. Marshal came from a line of minor officials who served in the court of King Henry I of England. Dubbed as a knight at the age of 20, he made his reputation and a good living fighting in tournaments. Marshal became a companion to King Henry II's youthful heir-apparent Henry, known as the Young King. When Henry fell sick, he asked Marshal to fulfill a deathbed wish to go on Crusade. Marshal spent two years fighting in Syria. On return he entered the service of the Young King's father, Henry II, and was rewarded with the promise of marriage to an heiress. The marriage was confirmed by Richard Lion-Heart after Henry II's death, and it made Marshal a wealthy man.

TOP LEFT: **The death of Richard I in France in 1199.**

ABOVE: **An engraving of the model English knight William Marshal, from his tomb in the Temple Church in London.**

When Marshal's elder brother died, he also inherited the Marshal family estate and the office of king's marshal. His star continued to rise through the reign of King John. He fulfilled important diplomatic missions during the later Angevin campaigns and served as regent for Henry III after the death of John. Marshal joined the Knights Templars before his death in 1219, thereby fulfilling all the requisites of a model knight.

The Mongol Hordes

Mounted warfare of the type that epitomized knighthood reached its peak in Europe during the Mongol invasions of the 13th century. In 1206, the legendary Mongol leader Genghis Khan united Mongolia's Asiatic tribes and sparked Mongol ambitions for world domination. His legacy was an unstoppable army of mounted archers. After storming Beijing in 1215, the Mongols completed domination of China in 1234. The next goal was the Russian tribes. The large numbers of cavalry — in excess of 100,000 — used in Mongol attacks gave birth to the phrase "Mongolian hordes." Disciplined and adaptable, the Mongols taught themselves siege techniques and attacked in winter when it was easy to travel rapidly on horseback across frozen marshland.

Genghis's grandson Batu Khan set his sights on Europe. European knights tried to mobilize themselves to repel the impeding Mongol threat, and the Church preached Crusades against them. The Mongol attack against Poland and Hungary began in 1241. Adept at ruses like feigned flight and encirclement, the Mongols were relentlessly victorious, pushing almost as far west as Vienna. Then word came that the leader of this Asian tribe was dead, and Mongol troops went home to choose a successor. The Mongol Empire deteriorated into factions, and its soldiers never returned to complete what seemed at the time like the inevitable defeat of Europe.

Robert the Bruce

The Scottish king Robert I, known as Robert the Bruce, provides another kind of real-life knightly exemplar. After initially supporting the rule of English King Edward I over Scotland, Robert fought hard for Scottish independence from 1297 to 1302, once he saw the oppressive nature of English rule there. His coronation in 1307 occurred after he had murdered his rival, and he was forced to take refuge in the countryside as a result. According to a story that circulated during those dark times, watching the perseverance of a spider spinning a web inspired Robert not to despair. Through guerrilla warfare, Robert eventually consolidated his hold on Scotland, dismantling English-held castles and defeating a large force of

LEFT: **A scene from the Battle of Bannockburn: the lightly-armed King Robert avoids the charge of Henry de Bohun and fells him with a blow from his axe.**

the English in the Battle of Bannockburn. In the 1328 Treaty of Northampton, the English finally recognized Scottish independence. Before Robert died in 1329, he requested that his heart be buried in Jerusalem. The knight entrusted with it was killed in Spain by Moors, so it was returned to Scotland and buried at Melrose Abbey.

The Hundred Years' War

One of the most infamous conflicts in the later years of knighthood was the Hundred Years' War, and it marked a significant series of changes in the conduct of knightly warfare. It was actually an intermittent series of clashes between England and France that spread into Flanders and the Iberian Peninsula. Hostilities began in 1337 when England's King Edward III tried to assume the French throne. The cause of the dispute lay in friction between the two countries that dated from William the Conqueror's defeat of the English at Hastings in 1066. Using dismounted knights flanked by archers, Edward bested the French in 1346 at the Battle of Crécy, one of the period's best-known engagements.

The English longbow, developed in England during the 13th century, gave the English army dominance at Crécy. Six feet long and made of imported yew wood, it shot a three-foot arrow. With a range of 400 yards, the longbow was twice as effective as the crossbow. It also was a lighter weapon, easier to handle and more adaptable. The longbow's one drawback was that it required years of training to use properly. English archers wiped out the Genoese crossbowmen employed by the French, and more than 1,500 French knights and nobles were killed at Crécy. In addition to the longbow, English naval power played an important role in the Hundred Year's War.

ABOVE: **English King Edward III defeats the French at the Battle of Crécy in 1346.**

In 1415, the French suffered a second notorious defeat at Agincourt in the hands of King Henry V of England. As they were at Crécy, Henry's forces were outnumbered three to one, but the French strategy of using cavalry to disperse the English archers misfired. The French forces came from traditional feudal levies and lacked the discipline of the more professional English knights, who fought for pay by indenture, or contract. Unable to defeat the English, the French knights surrendered, and Henry ordered most of them executed. His soldiers-at-arms refused to do the deed, and the 3,000 heavily armed French knights were killed by English archers, who aimed at their heads. The recurrent fighting between English and French forces destroyed the French countryside, depleted its population and fostered famine and the Plague. By the time it ended in 1453, the Hundred Years' War had also exhausted English resources and ended English domination in Europe.

Bertrand du Guesclin & Joan of Arc

Two French knights from the period also achieved legendary status. Bertrand du Guesclin exemplified the attributes of knighthood in the 14th century, and Joan of Arc was the only woman ever to achieve stature as a knight. Both were responsible for shifting the tide of English victories in favor of the French during the Hundred Years' War. Like William Marshal, du Guesclin did not come from royal blood or serve as a ruler. Knighted at the age of 34 in 1354, he concentrated on hit-and-run skirmishes against the English in the style of a guerrilla fighter. His clever tactics during an engagement at Rennes duped the Duke of Lancaster into leaving his camp unprotected. Du Guesclin promptly plundered it, but later demonstrated his chivalry by allowing the duke to enter Rennes long enough to plant his banner and withdraw. In 1364 du Guesclin subdued the Spanish forces of Charles of Navarre, who was trying to challenge the King of France. Captured by the English the same year, du Guesclin was ransomed by King Charles V and fought in his service until he died. Starting in 1370, he recaptured Poitou and Santage from the English and chased them into Brittany. He died in 1380 while campaigning in Languedoc. Du Guesclin's career as a knight was distinguished by his concern for the men who fought under him, his courage and his loyalty.

TOP: **John Fastolf was the best-known English knight in the Hundred Years' War as well as the model for Shakespeare's famous comic character Falstaff.**

BELOW: **A scene from Agincourt, where English longbowmen defeated the heavily armored French knights.**

ABOVE: **The Maid of Orleans,
Joan of Arc, defeats the English
at Patay in 1429.**

Daughter of a farmer, Joan of Arc, known as the Maid of Orleans, was deeply religious. She was guided to her calling as a knight by saintly voices. Her spiritual messengers, St. Margaret, St. Catherine and St. Michael, advised her to aid Charles VII, the French dauphin or royal heir, who had been kept from the throne by the English. With the aid of the military leader Robert de Baudricourt, Joan won an audience with the dauphin and went to it dressed in male clothing. She provided him with a sign of her mission's sanctity and was given troops, but not before suspicions of heresy were quelled by religious examination. In 1429 she rescued Orleans, under siege by the English, and defeated them at Patay. When Charles was crowned at Rheims Cathedral, Joan, who had urged his ascension to the throne, stood beside him. Her siege of Paris in 1429 was unsuccessful and she was later captured at Compiègne by rival Burgundian forces, who sold her to the English. Her trial in the court of the inquisition at Rouen for blasphemy and sorcery, as well as the cutting of her hair and wearing of men's clothes, added a tragic chapter to the history of knighthood. Joan's persecution had more to do with her gender than it did with her religious convictions or politics. She was burned at the stake in 1431. Her sometime benefactor Charles VII had her sentence annulled in 1456, and she was canonized as a saint in 1920. The story of her heroism and ordeals has been told many times, in works by such authors as Mark Twain, George Bernard Shaw and Jean Anouilh.

The best-known knight on the English side of the Hundred Years' War was the somewhat comical John Fastolf. The complexities of his career reflect the qualities typically found in 15th century knights. Coming from a middle class family of merchants and serving under contract, Fastolf distinguished himself

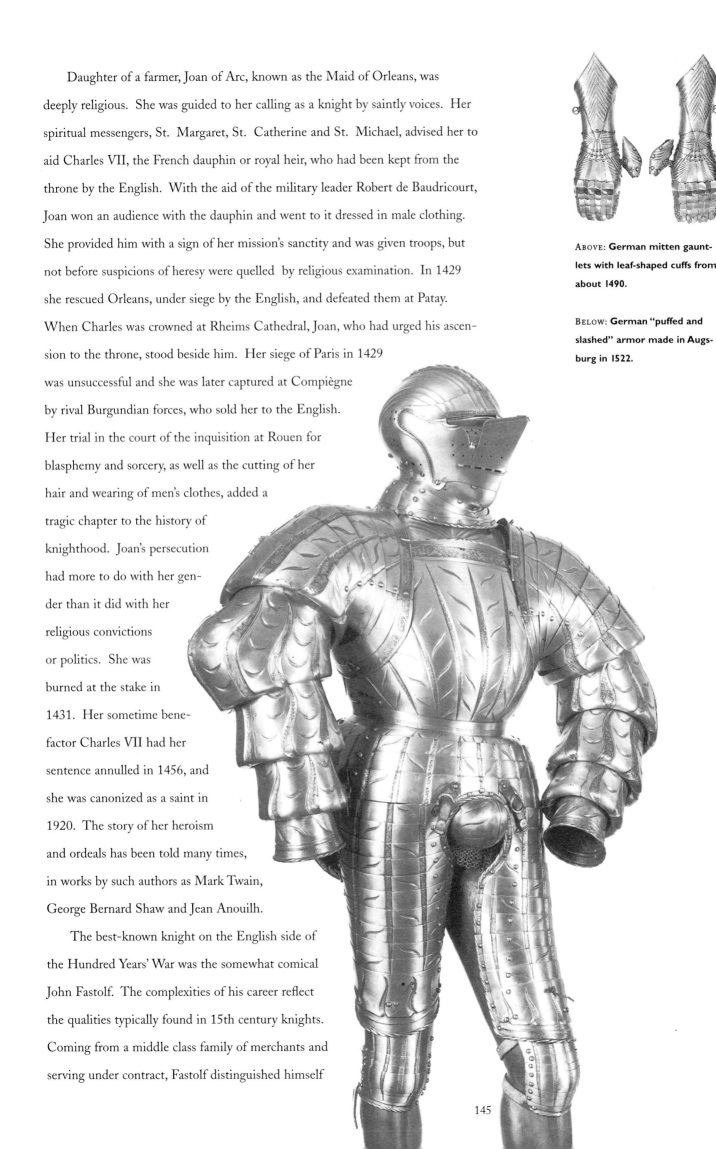

ABOVE: **German mitten gauntlets with leaf-shaped cuffs from about 1490.**

BELOW: **German "puffed and slashed" armor made in Augsburg in 1522.**

during the Battle of Agincourt and was knighted in 1418 at the age of 37. In 1425 he was installed as a Knight of the Garter, the order started by King Edward III in imitation of the Arthurian Round Table. He was notorious for his victory at the Battle of Herrings in 1429. While carrying supplies to Orleans during its siege, Fastolf was attacked there by a large number of French soldiers. He defeated them by using the barrels of herring he was transporting as a barri-cade. Present at the English rout by Joan of Arc at Patay, Fastolf was both praised for his pragmatism and vilified for cowardice. When he died in 1459, Fastolf had become a rich man from his military career and commercial interests. He provided the model for Shakespeare's most famous comic character, Falstaff, who appears in *Henry IV, Part I* and *Part II*, and *The Merry Wives of Windsor.*

The Advent of Plate Armor

By the middle of the 14th century, knights' armor began to evolve from mail into plate. Although plate armor was heavier than mail, it more successfully deflected lances, sword points, arrows and other missiles. Cuirasses, or breast-plates, made of hardened leather and worn either over or under a mail hauberk, or tunic, had come into fashion during the 13th century. The first step in the transition to plate armor was the plate coat, a cloth or leather tunic to which rectangular iron plates had been riveted in vertical rows. Such plates were also used to rein-force protective coverings for other vulnerable parts of the body like elbows, knees, throats, thighs, shins, arms and shoulders. Most of the knights who fought at the Battle of Crécy wore plate coats with hauberks under-neath. Plate armor was virtually indestructible and could be passed on from father to son. A blacksmith repaired what damage occurred during battle or jousting, and armor plates could be tinned or coppered to prevent rusting. The aventail was a series of plates that fanned out from the basinet, or helmet, to cover the neck and throat. A variation

on the plate coat was the brigantine, body
armor where the plates overlapped to
make the armor more flexible. A
cloth tunic known as coat
armor functioned as a way to
display a knight's coat of arms.

Centers for the manufacture of
armor which appeared in Germany and
in Italy led to distinctive Germanic and Italianate
styles. The German armorers developed a Gothic
style characterized by attenuated lines, while the
Italians used plainer and rounder designs. The two
styles of armor were blended into a new, hybrid form produced in Flanders. A knight's arms came to be protected
by a form of armor called bracers, which consisted of spaudlers
for the shoulder, rerebraces for the upper arm, couters for the elbow
and vambraces for the lower arm. Gauntlets grew narrower, with
cuffs that reached to the elbow. The sabatons used to protect a knight's feet became
exaggeratedly pointed, and some were removable to allow a knight to fight on foot.

New helm styles that emerged in the 15th century included the Italianate
armet, a visored, close-fitting headpiece, and the German sallet, a modification of
the kettle hat, which often had a tail that reached almost to the shoulders. A bevor,
protective covering for the chin and face, was usually worn with the sallet. The
celata was an Italian helmet with a rounded skull and keel-shaped comb that went

Top: A grotesque helmet made for Henry VIII by the armorer to German king Maximilian I.

Above: A full suit of plate armor made in Milan around 1455.

Left: The globular basinet on the effigy of Sir Hugh Despenser shows how the aventail, or curtain of mail, is attached to the helmet.

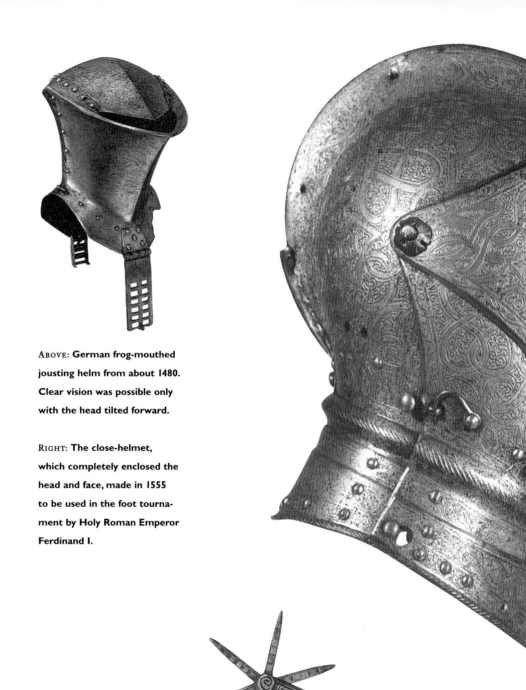

ABOVE: German frog-mouthed
jousting helm from about 1480.
Clear vision was possible only
with the head tilted forward.

RIGHT: The close-helmet,
which completely enclosed the
head and face, made in 1555
to be used in the foot tournament by Holy Roman Emperor
Ferdinand I.

ABOVE: A knight's gilt-metal
rowel spur.

LEFT: A German visored sallet,
black with painted decoration,
from about 1490.

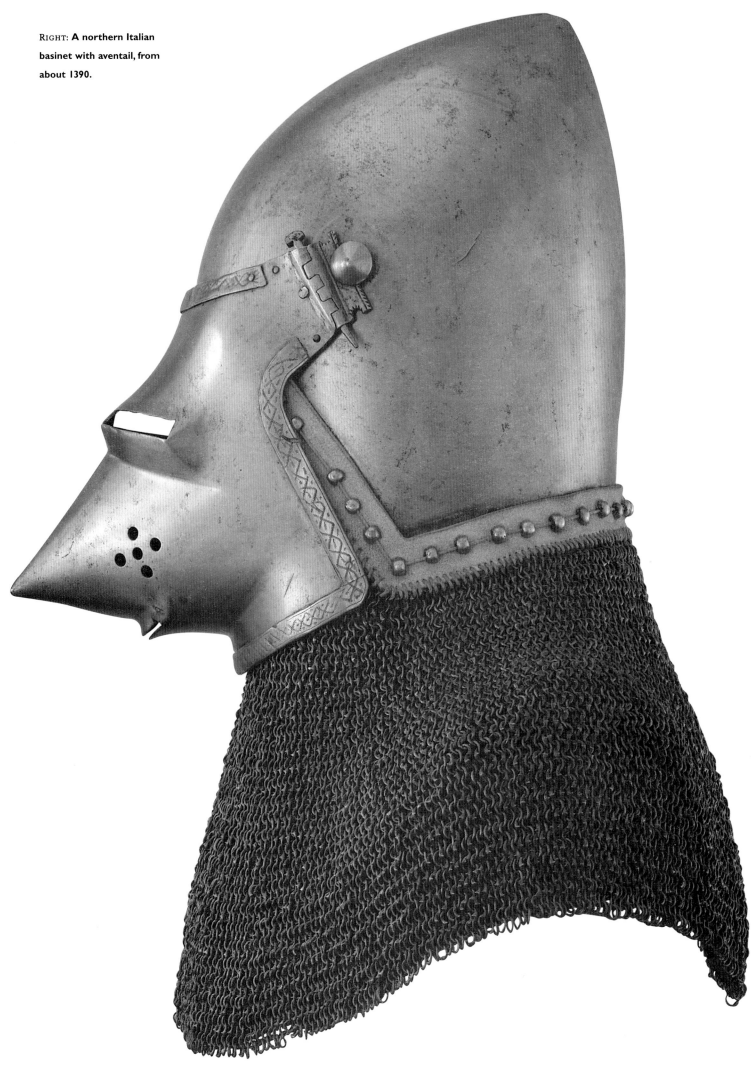

RIGHT: **A northern Italian basinet with aventail, from about 1390.**

to the nape of the neck. The German Kastenbrust was a new type of solid breastplate that sloped out and down from the chest, cutting in at the waist. A fauld, armor to protect the abdomen, was attached to it.

At the same time that plate armor began to be adopted, spurs changed, evolving from simple pricks to the rowel. Instead of a single spike, the rowel spur had a wheel of spikes. It continued to be used long after the age of knighthood ended.

A serious problem that developed with the advent of plate armor was heat exhaustion. By the time a knight suited up in a padded aketon, hauberk and plate coat, he was heavily insulated. White armor, which was fully plated, developed in part to alleviate the overheating that felled all too many knights. Armor also became more heavily decorated, with fluting particularly popular. Fluting imitated the folds or pleating on cloth garments, similar to the way folds appear on classical sculpture. Armor was rarely painted, but it was often etched or embossed starting in the 15th century. The heavily quilted coat called the gambeson or aketon became increasingly popular as a thrifty alternative to mail hauberks. Jewels, precious metals and sumptuous fabrics often enhanced helmets and body armor. Armor also had to be cleaned and oiled regularly, with olive oil the most common substance used. In aesthetic terms, the manufacture of armor reached its apogee in the 16th century. But in many ways, the 15th century set a more important standard of excellence, since the goal then was to achieve beauty through function.

150

CHAPTER 10

The Twilight of Knighthood

By the end of the 15th century, knighthood was being transformed by major changes. The rising cost of equipping and maintaining oneself as a knight limited the number of individuals who undertook its rigorous training. Pillaging and booty became inadequate as a reimbursement, and the practice of scutage, in which vassals were levied a tax in lieu of military service to finance specific campaigns, drained resources. Those that did become knights increasingly expected to be paid. Knighthood underwent a professionalization that resulted in more disciplined, consistent service. The earliest record of a military contract in England, which led the change to paid military service, dates from 1213. Lord Robert of Berkeley committed himself to serve in France with ten knights to repay a royal debt of 500 marks. By 1287, a similar contract even enumerated the value of the horses provided by a knight. The campaigns of the Hundred Years' War necessitated elaborate contracts that included the length of service, the number of knights supplied, their ranks and their rates of pay. Once contracts for military services came into existence, knighthood underwent a democratization, since the greatest leaders no longer necessarily came from the nobility. Professionalization of knighthood slowly disengaged it from the high ideals of chivalry, as Henry V's slaughter of the French knights who surrendered at Agincourt illustrated. Instead, more superficial elements of chivalry were practiced at tournaments, where etiquette and ostentation became the rule. At its height, knighthood depended on fast-moving cavalry, but as armor for knights and their horses became increasingly heavy and cumbersome, the advantage of mounted troops declined. The use of infantry in combination with cavalry increased, and knights often dismounted to fight on foot during engagements.

The Hussite Rebellion

Nationalism also changed the face of war. In Bohemia, now Czechoslovakia, the followers of John Hus, a religious reformer who was burnt at the stake in 1415, distinguished themselves through the nationalist nature of their rebellion

BELOW: **A billman from the period of the Wars of the Roses wears a north Italian brigandine, a cloth jacket with many metal plates riveted inside.**

OPPOSITE: **The crown is offered to the Earl of Richmond, later Henry VII, after his defeat of Richard III at Bosworth Field.**

against German authority. In 1420, they promulgated the Four Articles of Prague, calling for freedom to preach, communion for laymen, limits on Church property, and civil punishment for mortal sins. They expelled King Sigismund of Hungary and conducted a series of raids on Germany. The Germans never succeeded in subduing the Hussites, despite several Crusades against them.

The Hussites hold an important place in the annals of knighthood, in part because they developed a tactic known as the wagenburg, or wagon castle. It relied on the use of wagons, which the Hussites chained together into a circle or square called a laager as a defense against cavalry charges. The wagenburg can be thought in some ways to be a predecessor to the modern tank. The Hussites eventually defeated themselves through internal dissension, somewhat like the Mongols who had preceded them.

In part of the larger move toward the professionalization of knighthood, Italy in the 14th century produced the condottieri, professional cavalrymen who hired themselves out to fight in the economic wars between the Italian cities. Unlike other military forces of the time, they did not disperse at the end of a campaign but acquired discipline through consistent service. Their method of organization spread to Germany, England and then France. The most famous condottieri came from

the Sforza, Colleoni and Carmagnola families. The English knight Sir John de Hawkwood also won fame as one. Although the condottieri initially presented an imposing martial force, their effectiveness eventually deteriorated because their leaders were reluctant to risk the lives of the troops who provided their livelihood.

Swiss mercenaries rose to preeminence as the first truly national army. Because they inhabited a small country where soldiers needed to return quickly to their agricultural responsibilities, the Swiss never took prisoners or booty. Fighting as infantrymen in traditional Germanic squares, they wielded pikes or halberds — six-to-ten-foot pikes topped with axheads — which could fracture armor or drag a knight off his horse. The rules of chivalry were not important to the Swiss, and they killed men, women and children without discrimination. In 1315 Swiss infantrymen expelled the German Hapsburgs and won their independence, demonstrating the effectiveness of foot soldiers against mounted knights. They soon began contracting their services to other countries and improved the Swiss economy through their work as mercenaries. A related form of mercenary force in the 15th century were the Landsknechte, which copied Swiss tactics and were organized into units by region. The Landsknechte were employed in a number of German conflicts and traveled accompanied by a large retinue of women and servants.

The Advent of Gunpowder

Gunpowder dealt the decisive blow to traditional knighthood. It arrived in Europe during the middle of the 13th century but didn't become effectual until the 14th century. Initially the weaponry employing gunpowder was inaccurate, short in range, slow to fire, heavy, awkward and unreliable. As they evolved, the new weapons proved increasingly lethal. Firearms eliminated the protective advan-

TOP LEFT: **In a 15th-century drawing, Swiss infantry armed with pikes and other hafted arms repel attacking cavalry.**

ABOVE: **The Bohemian religious reformer John Hus (d. 1415).**

tage of armor as well as the distinctions between knights and ordinary soldiers.

The handgun first appeared in the 14th century as part of the infantry soldier's arsenal. The earliest versions looked like miniature cannons mounted to wooden shafts. A soldier tucked one under his arm, lit the powder and hoped the weapon did not explode in his face. Two popular 15th-century versions of handguns were the hackbut and arquebus. The matchlock musket, which replaced them, was up to seven feet long and fired ten-pound shot, but could only function in dry weather. The wheel-lock gun, developed in the 16th century, used a piece of iron pyrite to generate igniting sparks in conjunction with a revolving, serrated wheel. The matchlock gun of the 15th century, however, was cheaper, sturdier, easier to use and continued to predominate.

Cannons, which fired stones or iron balls, emerged as valuable weapons for sieges, as much for the panic they caused as the damage they inflicted. The earliest mention of cannons came in a Florentine authorization for their manufacture in 1326. The first versions of them were called pots-de-fer, vasili and sclopi. Wheeled artillery known as ribauldequins appeared by the end of the 14th century. Another new siege weapon was the bombard, a giant, muzzle-loaded gun. It also went by a variety of other names — falcons, sakers, cuverain, basilisk, veuglaries and couleuvrines — and fired shot weighing up to 300 pounds. In contrast to its predecessor the bow and arrow, the gun required less training to use and fired a missile that was heavier and more disabling. The development of this type of weaponry set off some of the earliest arms races in history and sometimes brought the kings and nobles who participated close to bankruptcy.

Wars of the Roses & Charles the Bold

The great era of knighthood drew to a close in the 15th century with the Wars of the Roses in England and the campaigns of Charles the Bold of Burgundy. In the Wars of the Roses, two English families, the Lancasters and the Yorks, fought over the throne from 1455 to 1485. The Lancasters, whose symbol was a red rose, had produced three kings: Henry IV, Henry V and Henry VI. Under the leadership of Richard, the York faction, whose symbol was a white rose, contested the rule of Henry VI. The Yorks prevailed at the Battle of St. Albans in 1455. After Richard fell in a battle against forces mustered by Henry VI's wife, Queen Margaret, contests continued between the two factions. Then another Richard from the York family won the upper hand. He became King Richard III, notorious for his ruthless ambition and deformed physique. After Richard was killed in battle, Henry VII became king and united the Houses of York and Lancaster by marrying Edward IV's daugh-

ABOVE: **A woodcut of a German mercenary, or Landsknecht, of the late 15th century.**

ter Elizabeth. The prolonged fighting of the Wars of the Roses, which exhausted the ranks of nobility, marked the end of knighthood in England.

On the continent, Charles the Bold contested the authority of France's new king, Louis XI. Charles controlled the Netherlands, Belgium and Luxembourg, as well as Burgundy and other parts of France. His attacks on Alsace and Lorraine antagonized the Swiss, who roundly defeated him, and he died at their hands in Nancy in 1476. Charles's ambitious plans to establish a new kingdom died with him, and Burgundy was absorbed by France, never existing again as a separate state. Although Charles had adapted modern military tactics, using professional soldiers in a combination of cavalry, infantry and artillery, he could not overcome the Swiss.

By the 16th century, the size of armies increased dramatically, along with the cost of making war. Experts argue over whether the changes in warfare that rendered the knight obsolete by the 16th century were revolutionary or evolutionary. What remains clear is that knighthood continues to have a profound and inspirational impact on the world. Most memorable are its use of armor and horses to enhance individual force, its rituals and, most of all, its ideals. Embodied in the knight's code of chivalry, these ideals attempted to bring order and give meaning to the terrible forces of combat.

Index

Numbers in *italics* indicate illustrations

Acknowledgments

The publisher would like to thank the following
people who helped prepare this book:
Beth Crowell of Cheung/Crowell Design, the
designer; Sara Dunphy, the picture researcher;
Jean Martin and Margaret Sobel, the editors;
and Elizabeth Miles Montgomery, the indexer.

Picture Credits

Archive Photos/Kean Archives: pages 15
    (bottom), 35, 36, 57 (top), 68 (both), 69
    (all three), 87, 92 (top left), 97, 124 (top left),
    129.
Aufnahme des Kunsthistorischen Museums:
    page 145 (bottom).
James Austin Photography: page 84.
Bibliotheque Nationale: pages 27, 79 (bottom),
    86, 121, 122, 127 (top), 128 (bottom), 134
    (bottom), 136, 137, 143 (bottom), 144 (top).
The Board of Trustees of The Armouries: pages
    77, 95, 96 (top), 100 (both), 124 (bottom),
    128 (top), 131, 132, 145 (top right), 146
    (bottom left), 147 (top), 148 (top left, center,

bottom left), 149, 150, 151, 152, 156.
Bodleian Library, Oxford: page 80 (both).
The British Library: pages 40, 55, 57 (bottom),
    62, 72, 73 (top), 79 (top), 90, 93, 101,
    106 (top left), 114, 116, 123 (bottom), 125,
    126, 142.
© British Museum: pages 11 (top), 13 (top), 65,
    78, 98 (bottom).
Brompton Picture Library: pages 3, 5, 22, 60,
    66, 109, 133 (bottom left), 135 (bottom
    right), 155 (bottom right).
Burgerbibliothek, Bern: page 155 (top left).
Corbis-Bettmann: pages 1, 2, 4, 7, 8 (top),
    11 (bottom), 12, 16 (top), 19, 20 (bottom),
    21, 23 (both), 24, 25, 26, 28, 29, 30, 32
    (both), 33, 37, 38 (top), 39, 42, 43, 44, 45, 46,
    51, 52, 58 (bottom), 61 (top), 63, 64, 70, 71,
    73 (bottom), 74, 75, 76, 77 (top), 81 (top
    right), 83, 85, 89, 91, 94 (top left), 98 (top
    left), 104, 105, 106 (bottom), 107, 108, 111,
    112 (both), 113, 115 (top right), 117- 120,
    127 (bottom right), 130, 133 (top right),
    135 (top left), 138, 139 (both), 140 (top left),
    143 (top right), 143 (bottom left), 153.
The Dean and Chapter of Durham: page 99.
Deutschen Archaologischen Instituts, Rome:
    page 13 (bottom).
Germanisches Nationalmuseum, Nurnberg:
    page 154.
Glasgow Museums: Art Gallery & Museum,
    Kelvingrove: page 147 (bottom right); The
    Burrell Collection: page 41.
Heidelberg University Library: page 61
    (bottom).
Hulton Getty Collection: pages 9, 10, 31, 48
    (bottom), 50, 56, 58 (top), 59 (both), 88,
    92 (bottom), 94 (bottom), 103, 110, 140.
Image Select/Ann Ronan Picture Library:
    page 67.
MAS, Barcelona: pages 20 (top), 53.
Musees Royaux des Beaux-Arts de Belgique,
    Bruxelles: page 123 (top right).
The Museum of London: pages 15 (top), 82.
National Army Museum, London: page 157.
National Museum, Copenhagen, Denmark:
    pages 34, 48 (top).
National Museum of Iceland: page 49.
New College, Oxford/Photo Courtesy The
    Bridgeman Art Library, London: page 6.
Royal Commission on the Historical Monuments
    of England: page 147 (bottom left).
© Stiftsbibliothek, St. Gallen, Switzerland:
    pages 14, 38 (bottom).
© Trustees of the National Museums of Scotland:
    page 81 (left).
Trustees of the Winchilsea Settled Estates, Photo
    Courtesy Northamptonshire County Council:
    page 115 (bottom left).
University Library, Gottingen: page 54.
University of London: Conway Library,
    Courtauld Institute of Art: page 96 (bottom);
    The Warburg Institute: page 8 (bottom).
University of Oslo, University Museum of
    National Antiquities: page 18.
Ville de Paris, Musee du Petit Palais, Collection
    Dutuit © Phototheque des Musees de la Ville
    de Paris: page 11 (top).
The Wallace Collection: page 148 (top right).
Zentrabibliothek, Zurich: page 102.